Techniques in

Kathleen Kinder

Techniques in Machine Knitting

Kathleen Kinder

PHOTOGRAPHS BY GEORGE KINDER

Arco Publishing, Inc.
New York

For George, Edmund, and Helen

Published 1985 by Arco Publishing, Inc.
215 Park Avenue South, New York, NY 10003

© Kathleen Kinder
First published 1983

Library of Congress Cataloging in Publication Data

Kinder, Kathleen, 1932–
    Techniques in machine knitting.

    Bibliography: p.
    1. Knitting, Machine. II. Title.
TT680.K527   1985   746.43'2   84–12400
ISBN 0–668–06285–1

Printed in Great Britain

Contents

Acknowledgements

My grateful thanks to Andrea Whitley for typing the script and for her expert advice. I am indebted to the importers and manufacturers of knitting machines for their continued support and help so freely and willingly given. Thanks are also due to John Millington, editor/managing director of *Knitting International*, to Hazel Ratcliffe, editor/publisher of *Knitting Machine Digest*, for permission to use in this book parts of my articles on lace knitting in their publications, and to Simon Tuite of Batsford for patient forbearance and cheerful encouragement.

To Dr Stanley Chapman, Department of Economic History, Nottingham University, from whose copies of *The History of the Machine Wrought Hosiery and Lace Manufacturers*, William Felkin (1867), and the *History of the Framework Knitters*, Gravenor Henson (1831), I have quoted. Both are David & Charles reprints.

The International Wool Secretariat (Technical Division Library); The Rachel Kay-Shuttleworth Collection, Gawthorpe Hall, Burnley, Lancashire; Knitmaster (Modern Knitting) Ltd; *Knitting International* (Leicester); The National Museum of Antiquities (Edinburgh); North Yorkshire County Library Services; Nottingham University Library (special collections); The Pasold Fund; Textile History; The Ulster Museum, Belfast; The Victoria & Albert Museum, London.

All other work is by the author unless otherwise credited.

Introduction

Machine knitting is a textile craft extraordinaire. It has developed, under the silence of textile craft authorities, to the point where it has captured the interest and enthusiasm of a dedicated and growing band of people who represent a wide cross-section of the community. Machine knitting suits the temperament of our day and age. To be able to produce a garment or article within the time allotted is not only healing therapy but ultimate satisfaction. Contrary to what many people think, machine knitting is not a new craft but a modern manifestation of the oldest form of the knitter's craft – peg-frame knitting. It has its own fascinating, tumultuous history and inherits a dual tradition from hand and mechanised knitting.

Because so much of the framework of machine-knitting has been ignored by handicraft scholars, and because all things new have their roots in all things old, I give historical as well as technical background. For the original research which forms the basis of the historical study, please see 'The history of knitting and the knitting machine' in my *Resource Book for Machine Knitters* published under copyright in 1979. It is good to report that the influence of the anti-machine movement in the crafts is receding, and that people are at last realising that a whole complex area of skills and a satisfying relationship with tools are involved with machine-knitting. The definition of a handicraft as a manual pursuit with the maximum handling of raw material is both inadequate and spurious. In this area at least, the influence of William Morris and of his Arts & Crafts movement in the nineteenth century has not been a good one.

As far as machine knitting is concerned, people are now bold enough to say how much they enjoy their machines and how rewarding is the mastery. With the enjoyment, the inhibitions and fear of mechanical tools disappear. This, perhaps more than any other reason, is why more and more people are taking up the craft. There is at least one machine on the market to suit every taste, interest and level of achievement.

It is strange to think that both hand and machine knitting have had an almost entirely down-to-earth, functional past. Even the famous knitted carpets, ancestors of the currently popular picture knitting, were produced as part of an exacting examination process for admission to the eighteenth century guilds of Europe. These carpets were not commissioned as objets d'art by a patron. For the new fibre artists – machine knitters therefore, there is very little precedent to depart from or to follow. Some rely heavily on modern hand knitting or on the traditions of the weaving craft. A few need to be reminded that the machine knitting craft has its own discipline and rules. Others are breaking out into the new ground of an undiscovered country.

I continue to present the approach of my previous writing, the concept of the total craft, using several makes of machine to suit a wide variety of tastes and interests. Though you may not wish to knit all the patterns in the book, please study them for the techniques they contain and then try these techniques out on articles of your own choosing. I find great inspiration in the demonstrable belief of the Renaissance that the way to excellence lies through the unity of the creative imagination with the discipline of technical perfection. The two must be kept in harmony if the end product is to be of lasting worth and an enrichment to our lives. I hope, therefore, that whatever machine you possess you will feel that here is something for you to read, enjoy and knit.

The pattern format

The diagrams, where applicable, are given in the form they would appear on the charting device. Measurements are in centimetres first and inches second, and they too are given for the convenience of charting device owners, who may wish to copy the blocks onto paper or plastic sheet for use in the charting attachment with yarn of their own choice. The instructions for the Passap Duomatic follow second after those for the Japanese machines in the majority of patterns. The tensions on the Superba and Singer Electronic machines approximate to those on the Passap Duomatic stitch dial. The 10 cm readings for Passap, Superba and Singer Electronic owners will be found in the last chapter of this book (Fig. 196). Special instructions for Passap owners will also be found in my book, *The Passap Duomatic, Deco and Forma – Patterns and Comment for all Duomatics.*

Always knit a tension square in the manner suggested for your machine. The recommended stitch size in the pattern is less important than the stitch and row tension it achieves. Adjust the stitch dial either up or down if necessary. Read through the section on the brand names of machines at the back of the book if you are an overseas reader, to avoid possible confusion. Before you pattern knit, check through the abbreviations and read the instructions and pattern notes which follow after to make quite sure you have understood the procedures.

1 Stockings

For at least two thousand years, possibly longer, the knitter has been an accessory maker and not the creator of high fashion. The leap from this lowly estate did not take place till the 1920s, and Gabrielle 'Coco' Chanel is immortalised as the person who engineered the quite remarkable change of status for a society which at last required the knitter's fabric as the stuff of modern life.

The earliest pieces of knitted fabric extant were found on the site of the old Syrian city of Dura Europos, which was sacked by the Persians in A.D. 256 and then left to the preserving qualities of the desert sand.

From Egypt came some of the first recognisable articles to be found. Amongst these were Coptic sandal socks and a knitted cap, dated around the fourth or fifth century A.D., now in the collection of the Victoria and Albert Museum (Fig. 1). It is the socks which concern us here. Until Dorothy Burnham and her colleagues in the Royal Ontario Museum discovered that these articles were done by a one-needle technique, it was thought that they were executed by two needles in a knitting stitch called Eastern Cross-Stitch. By whatever technique these two-toed sandal socks were produced, the shaping of the article is of great interest to modern hand and machine knitters. The socks were open to the front instep and were meant to be laced. The shaping of the heel shows a sophisticated technique, which is very similar to that used by a modern hand knitter but not to the method used by the modern machine knitter.

In 1589 the Reverend William Lee of Calverton, near Nottingham, invented the hand frame, which was based on the ancient peg-frame principle of knitting. Initially, the frame's main purpose was to produce stockings, but many other articles of clo-thing, some of them of extraordinary beauty as well as utility, were produced during the golden years of the frame in the eighteenth century. Indeed, the few hand frames that remain are still world famous for the cobwebby, delicate shawls that belong to a tradition of lace knitting considerably older than that from Shetland.

Gravenor Henson, in his *History of the Framework Knitters* (1831), has a very interesting passage on p. 39 about how Lee wrestled with the problem of constructing a machine which would make a 'round web'. Lee did not succeed, of course; that honour was left for Brunel, some 227 years later. What Lee observed, however, was that the hand knitter changed from four needles to two needles in order to execute the heel. In the same way, the owner of a modern double bed machine changes from two beds to one to work the same processes. Henson describes the development of Lee's idea: 'The thought struck him instantly that he could make a flat web and then by joining the selvages with the needle make it round'.

Henson goes on to tell us how Lee grappled for months with the problem of turning the heel, but tells us nowhere how it was resolved. From a seventeenth century representation of the coat of arms of the London Framework Knitters' Guild, it is apparent that the heel was shaped in three separate sections, which were then seamed together (see Fig. 80). The modern domestic machines have the great advantage of the holding cam levers for shaping without bulk. The heel and the toe can be done in simple but fascinating operations on any modern domestic machine.

In the seventeenth century, knitters also began to apply embroidered clox or clocks to stockings, a

fashion which continued through to the nineteenth century and has enjoyed a recent revival in our own day (Figs 2 and 3). Because embroidery took so long to execute, Russian clox embroiderers used to cut off the embroidered areas from worn stockings and appliqué them to newly knitted ones. These techniques are worth studying and are early examples of mixed media craft – machine knitted articles adorned with embroidery and appliqué.

The early framework knitters took great pride in their work. In the first decades of the nineteenth century, when thousands of framework knitters were put out of work by speedier methods and new technology, it was their bitter complaint that 'cut and sew' stockings, the 'spurious articles' which had brought them to the brink of starvation, were 'not fashioned properly with selvages'.

Single Bed Socks

Though single bed socks must be seamed, they can be knitted in a greater variety of patterns than on the

Figure 1. Egypto–Roman socks, fourth–fifth century A.D. (Victoria and Albert Museum)

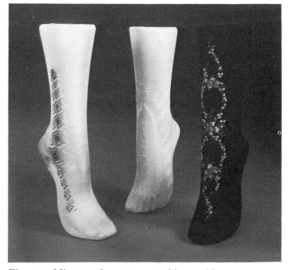

Figure 2. Nineteenth-century stockings with embroidered clox (Museum of Costume. Bath)

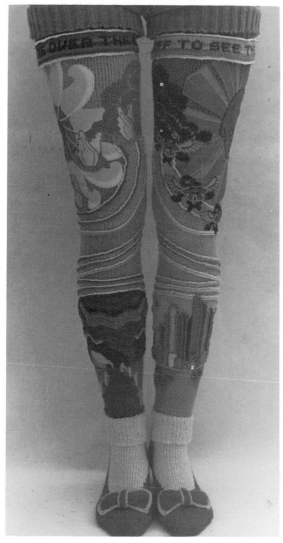

Figure 3. Oz Socks with crochet and appliqué, by Susanna Lewis, New York. (Knitted on a Passap Duomatic)

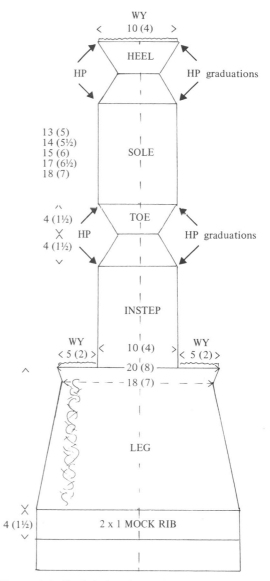

Figure 4(a). Single bed socks (back seam). N.B. Both socks are the same

double bed. Only the Passap Duomatic has patterning cams for circular knitting – DX for tubular tuck and HX for tubular slip or Fair Isle. Therefore, it is customary to see mainly stocking stitch patterns for stockings knitted 'in the round'. No modern domestic machine can rib in the round in the manner of the old circular sock machine. The single bed machine, however, provides the knitter with a variety of pattern settings from which to choose adornment for knitted stockings. Historically, self-coloured tuck 'ribs' were the first to be employed in the knitting of stockings on the hand frame, from about the 1740s till the invention of the rib-frame in the late 1750s.

Methods of knitting single bed stockings

There are two main methods of knitting single bed stockings.

1. With the seam at the back of the leg and two seams at the side of the foot (Fig. 4a). Because the embroidered Fair Isle clox in the sock pattern adorn the inside of the leg, the method employed is the back seam method. The girth of the foot is not as critical as the length, but where it is considered necessary to increase the girth it is increased by groups of four stitches, which are added to a total complement, also divisible by four.

At the division of the heel and the instep, two

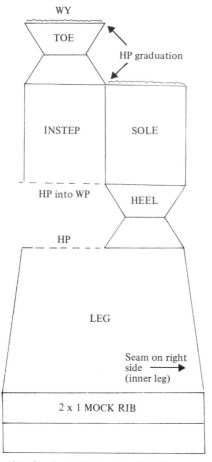

Figure 4(b). Single bed left sock with side seam. N.B. Reverse for right sock

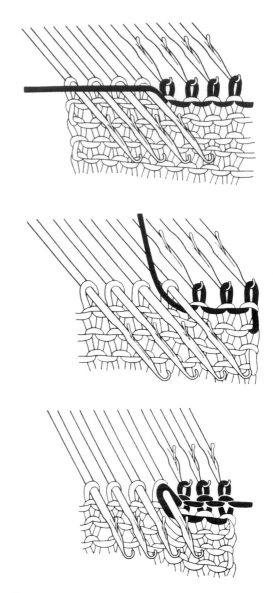

Figure 5. Shaping by holding position

quarters of the total complement of stitches are for the instep/sole, and two quarters, one at each side, are for the heel.

2. With the seam at the side of the leg and side of the foot (Fig. 4b). If the back of the leg is in full view, then of course, this method is more suitable than method 1. Moreover, there is only one continuous seam. It is important to point out that there is a right and left sock, because the seam is on the inside of the leg. The total complement of stitches needs only to be divisible by two.

Disadvantages of method 2

(a) No additional shaping, by a sudden increase, can be added easily to the heel, as in method 1.

(b) To be able to change methods in the same yarn and tension and to be able to turn a single bed pattern into a double bed one are useful advantages. Method 1 is more versatile than method 2 as a multi-purpose technique. It can also be adapted as a charting device pattern more easily than method 2.

A further point: When measuring girth of the leg or foot, do not allow any ease.

Mary Thomas's Knitting Book contains a most interesting and useful chapter on stocking knitting. Mary Thomas does not seem to operate under any discipline as far as the division of stitches is concerned. Indeed, there is no discernible rule for the instep and heel stitches, so maybe the machine knitter is being over-fastidious. Mary Thomas does, however, offer interesting suggestions for the strengthening of heel and toe. In this pattern, the heel and toe strengthener is nylon thread, knitted in with the main yarn. She tells the hand knitter to use slip stitch or knitweave and, certainly, the machine knitter could do likewise.

Peasant stocking knitting is a very ancient occupation. In the U.K. there were famous stocking markets at Bala in Wales and Kendal in Cumbria. The Aberdeen stocking knitters were mentioned by Dr Johnson, and the Channel Islands had established a lively export trade in knitted stockings by the end of the sixteenth century. Nevertheless, there is no doubt that many rural stocking knitters were some of the poorest in the land. Yorkshire Dales knitters knitted in the dark under the blankets when they could not afford heat and light. When Welsh knitters ran out of wool they omitted the toe section and knitted instead a narrow sling to anchor the sock over the big toe. The peasant stocking knitting of Central Europe and Scandinavia is some of the most colourful in the world. Not only were the stockings knitted in allover Fair Isle patterns, many of them were heavily embroidered as well. The ideas for the pattern in this book came from a variety of sources.

Lady's Embroidered Fair Isle Knee Socks

Size in cm
Completed length of foot: 20 (8), 22 (8½), 23 (9), 24 (9½), 25 (10) cm.
Completed length of leg: 32 (12½) cm.

Measurements
On drawing for Method 1 (Fig. 4a). Charting device users should copy only half of the shape to the right of the vertical dotted line.

Materials
Colour 1: 100 g (4 oz) (all sizes).
Colour 2: 20 g (1 oz) (all sizes).
Colour 3: a small amount of Swiss darning.
Nylon thread, cord elastic (optional).

Pattern
For punchcard machines and electronics. Norwegian sock pattern. 12 stitch repeat as punchcard.

Tension
MT 5 (Passap St S 4¾) 30 stitches – 42 rows per 10 cm. 13.4 cm – 14.3 cm per 40 stitches × 60 rows.

Machine used
Knitmaster 360.

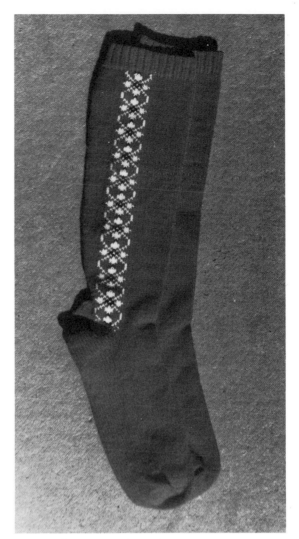

Figure 6. Embroidered Fair Isle socks

Socks
Push up 76 needles to WP (Passap owners, see note 3). Take third and every following third needle into NWP for single bed 2 × 1 mock rib. Using WY and MT cast on and knit 8 rows ending at right. Knit in nylon cord. Carr at left. Change to MY. RC 000, MT − 3, Knit 14 rows. Change to MT + 1, Knit 1 row. Change to MT − 3, knit 14 rows. On last row of rib, insert PC and lock on row 1. Complete double welt. Carr at right, RC 000. Change to MT. Arrange for Fair Isle and single motif knitting (see notes 2 and 3). Release punchcard. Inc 1 stitch at each end of next row (78 sts).

Left Sock
Motif panel between ns 13–24 (inclusive) at left of 0.

13

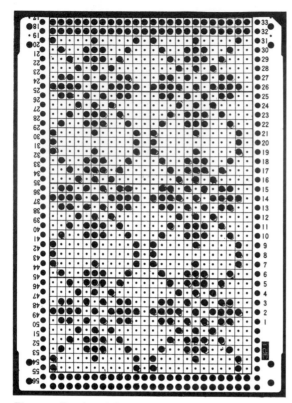

Figure 7. Punchcard for Fair Isle socks

Right sock

Motif panel between ns 13–24 (inclusive) at right of 0. Knit 21 rows straight. Dec 1 stitch ff using 2 eyed tool, at both ends of next and foll 18th row, 4 times in all. Knit 2 rows straight. Dec 1 stitch ff at both ends of next and foll 5th row, 8 times in all (54 sts). Knit 4 rows straight. RC 118. Inc 1 stitch at both ends of next 5 rows (64 sts) RC 123. Knit 3 rows straight. Carr at right. RC 126. Fasten off second colour. Change back to stocking st. Counting from left, push 48 ns to HP. Set carr to hold. (Passap – BX and pushers for graduations). Using WY, knit 8 rows over 16 sts at right. Release from machine. Push 16 ns at extreme left back into UWP knit 8 rows in WY. Release from machine. Work over remaining 32 sts. RC 000. Knit 54, (60, 66, 70, 76,) rows straight. Carr at right.

Shape toe

*Thread up nylon and place in feed with MY. Always taking yarn and thread round the first inside n in HP, push 1 n opposite carr end to HP on next 16 rows (see note 4). Always taking yarn and thread round first inside n in HP push 1 n opposite carr end back into UWP on next 16 rows *. Remove nylon thread. Cont in MY only. RC 000 knit 54, (6), 66, 70, 76) rows.

Shape heel

Work as for toe from * to *. Scrap off in WY (8 rows). Release from machine.

Making up

Neaten Fair Isle panels and Swiss darn stitches as shown. If wool, pin out to size and press, omitting rib welts, if used. If acrylic, a cool dry press is optional. Join leg seam. Graft 32 sts from back of heel to 32 sts at base of leg seam. Remove WY. Passap owners– stitch down rib-welt. Join side seam of foot. Press all seams according to yarn. Insert cord elastic in welts.

Notes

1. This pattern is a traditional Norwegian Fair Isle design for socks, but it occurred in European embroidery and in woven textiles before it appeared in knitting, as indeed did many Scandinavian, Shetland, and Fair Isle patterns. The Swiss darning is over the four stitches in the centre of the motif and over the one stitch separating each motif.

2. *Neatening the edges of single motif knitting.* There are different methods for closing the gaps that can appear between the two yarns at the edges of motif knitting. One of the most successful is to prepare two little balls of neatening yarn in the main yarn. On the carriage side begin with a slip knot and place it on the first stitch in MY adjacent to the last needle holding a stitch in the second colour. On each row, at the side nearest the carriage, lift up the neatening yarn from the second row below and see that it crosses the second colour (stranded towards the cambox) as you lift it onto an adjacent outward needle holding a MY stitch at the edge of a motif. In the Toyota instruction book the suggestion is to hook the yarn over two needles (Fig. 9). This is particularly useful on the J & B, Toyota and Singer punchcard machines where the patterning needles come to UWP. Whichever method is best for your machine, the object of the exercise is to ensure that the second colour on its return is linked by the neatening yarn and a hole is prevented. The inside should be as pleasing as the outside. Passap Duomatic owners – wind the neatening yarn on two pieces of flat card, open the beds and drop the wound cards between, once you have anchored the first loops safely.

This method, as utilitarian as it may seem, has considerable decorative and fibre art possibilities. Experiment with several colours of yarn hooked up, as you please, across basic knitweave. Knit lengths of multicoloured cord and hook these up across knitweave; tuck or slip for a more dramatic 3-D effect.

3. *Passap knitters.* Knit a 1 × 1 rib on st s $3\frac{1}{2}$ for 29

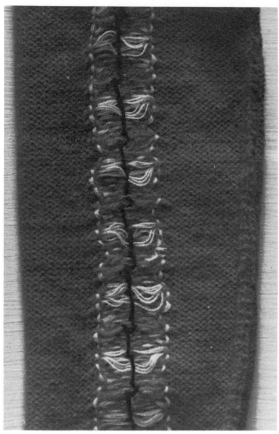

Figure 8. Inside the sock

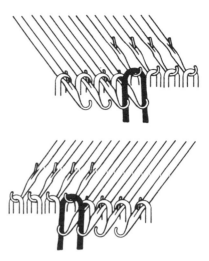

Figure 9. The Toyota method for neatening the edges of a motif

rows instead of a single bed welt. Do a fold row on R 15, using st s 5. Choose card 19 from your deco pack and make the motif 13 sts wide. Place the positioning pins to enclose the patterning area on single bed Fair Isle (Deco Instruction Manual p. 10). Alternatively, use a small based pattern with pushers. The socks of course can be knitted plain.

4. This pattern was knitted on the Knitmaster 360 KL, using the magic cams to enclose the motif area, which in this case is 12 sts wide. J & B, Singer and Toyota 901 owners should push back the needles outside the motif area, to normal WP. Toyota 787 and Knitmaster 321 owners – punch the card in reverse, and push back the needles not required. Because the pattern is 12 sts wide, it can also be put onto a card for the Toyota 747 machine, or pegged out on the Superba S44 pattern box.

5. There are two ways to shape the heel and toe by single stitch graduations:

(a) As per pattern, by pushing one needle opposite the carriage into HP. This needle must be wrapped on its return by the yarn and nylon being pulled down and round the needle to close the gap (Fig. 5);

(b) By pushing the needle nearest the carriage into HP. The needle does not need to be wrapped. This is a favourite method on the Passap Duomatic, where the operative cam is BX and a pusher is taken to RP as the equivalent of HP on the Japanese machines. The disadvantage of (b) is that it produces a flatter, less attractive fashioned look than (a), but the advantage is that (b) is quicker and less likely to produce problems when the knitter has to wrap a needle with nylon thread and yarn.

6. *Stitching a flat seam.* The best way for a flat finish is to overcast closely by hand, no more than one stitch in. For speed, and also for a flat finish, use a medium size zigzag on the sewing machine.

7. It may seem unusual to recommend the use of the charting device for socks and stockings, but why not? Many knitters want sock patterns, but cannot find them in the yarn they wish to use. Remember, the sole is the same length as the instep and any increase or decrease in even number of rows must take place on both. Similarly, any increases or decreases on the leg should take place evenly within the groups of rows designated for the shaping. It is also necessary to employ mental arithmetic to work out the graduations at heel and toe. Turn about half the width into graduations, a quarter at each side. The charting device is a marvellous aid. More and more knitters are wondering however they managed without it, but it still requires the support of the human calculator.

8. *Yarn tips.* $2 \times \frac{2}{16}$ English crossbred wool makes an excellent sock yarn, while cheap $\frac{2}{10}$ or $\frac{2}{8}$ oiled, industrial Shetland knitted throughout with nylon thread will surprise you for its hardwearing qualities.

2 Hats

In *Mrs Leach's Fancy Work Basket*, dated about 1887, there is an interesting child's cap in knitting and crochet called a 'fishwife's cap' and described as 'a tasteful little head dress, very easily made, most becoming and durable' (Fig. 10).

No such equivalent was offered to the ladies of the period, yet in 1959 adult readers of Knitmaster's *Modern Knitting* were offered machine knit patterns of 'pirate' caps almost identical to the children's versions of 80 years previously. The unisex ski-caps and the rib-tuck, double thickness head-huggers of modern times are obviously direct descendants, but knitted caps go back much further than the Victorian era.

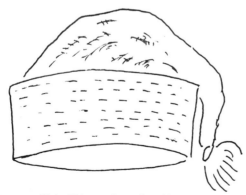

Figure 10. Fishwife's cap from the 1880s

A tiny cap knitted in fawn wool, dated around the third century A.D., was found in a Coptic burial in Egypt. It seems to have been made for a type of elfin Robin Hood, with shaping along the front peak and crown. Shaping of hats has always been a great challenge to knitters, although hats of the fishwife variety always managed to get by with the minimum of shaping. The knitter merely had to decrease the stitches along a 'pigtail' and finish it off with a tassel. The modern machine knitter knits the cap as one flat piece, does not bother with a pigtail and stitches up the one long seam to make a circular hat. Often the stitches are drawn together in a fullness on the crown and left to mould themselves to the head as best they can. The tassel or bobble is optional.

In early Tudor times the cappers' guilds were very important and influential. People of low estate were required by law to wear hats and the cappers' livelihood was assured. These hats were felted and shaped and were obviously the product of great skill. There are examples to be seen in the Museum of London. To make a knitted article fit and enhance a spherical object like the human head, the knitter is required to work out a system of complicated shapings. Berets and tams with turned-under brims and flattish crowns have always proved the most exacting to hand and machine knitters alike. When hats, berets and shaped babies' bonnets are in fashion the machine knitter employs the short row technique, which in itself is easy enough, but the secret lies in the calculations, how much to short row and how many stitches to leave unshaped to form the turned-under edge of a beret or the back piece of a bonnet. In the 1960s a flatter, less full beret was the fashion and the centre piece was knitted sideways to produce what looked like a large plate edged with a narrower, turned-under brim than one sees on pull-on berets of today. It is not easy to design a round beret. Trial and error are the only guides, but at least at the end of it there will be a healthy respect and admiration for the cap-knitters of a bygone age. They really knew how to make the knit-cap fit and look good at the same time.

Figure 11. Nineteenth century English children's caps.
(Victoria and Albert Museum)

During the Victorian period, baby and children's knitting reached a high peak of achievement. The younger generation could wear with approval the elastic fabric of the knitter which had not yet assumed the fashion status given to it by the twentieth century. Amongst the most beautiful and, indeed, the most impractical objects were the knitted caps (Fig. 11). Who, for example, would defy modern child care advice and dare to knit beads into a baby's bonnet? But, at least, there is plenty of inspiration in such exquisitely wrought, miniature headgear. It is useful to note how striking is the contrast afforded by beading, lace and the raised double-moss stitch pattern, which machine knitters can simulate with a popcorn tuck stitch. Indeed, tuck and lace combinations are already firm favourites with many machine knitters, and beaded knitting is also employed by those who want something special. On the cap on the left of the photograph the shaping has been cleverly directed into the segments of a beautiful star pattern along the crown, which provided the idea for the crown of the ski hat pattern in this book.

The Ski Hat Pattern

The chevron, which is the key motif, is of course one of the most ancient of all patterns used by man. Some of the earliest clay sherds are decorated with horizontal zigzags. The cap (Fig. 12) shows four developments of the zigzag in the machine-knit patterns, all of which fit onto a 60 row punchcard.

1. Every other needle Fair Isle is employed in the construction of the 1 × 1 mock welt. During the mid-1960s, when Knitmaster began to market the Japanese-made 302 machine, there was much promotion of the patterned single bed welt. Machine knitters of the period were more interested in acquiring a ribber in order to produce true ribs, but at least we can now return to the suggestions of 20 years ago and develop them without bias. The pattern is a 12 stitch repeat across 24 needles. The needle to the right of O must be in working position for the E O N pattern to work out correctly. If you choose the needle to the left of O as the pattern indicator, you will miss the vital connection and end up with a plain mock rib welt.

It is also important to recognise that rows one to four are in one colour i.e. colour two. Therefore, the

17

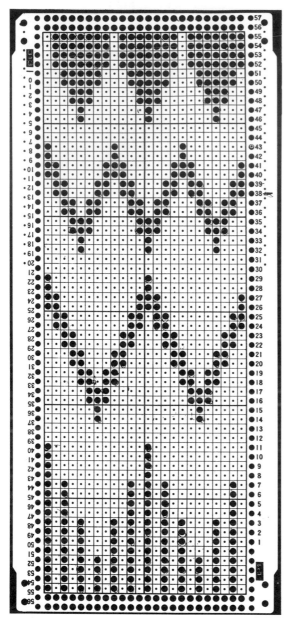

Figure 12. Punchcard for ski hat and mittens

be halted on a blank row, but this is not essential. On the Passap there is no need for any alternative. The colour changer provided with the machine is most efficient.

2. The chevron above the welt is also a twelve stitch repeat pattern, this time over all needles. Notice how it co-ordinates with the welt pattern. There are long-ish floats with this pattern. They are out of harm's way in a hat. If the pattern is organised for a smaller size, then this pattern is best omitted altogether.

3. The next pattern up the card is an eight stitch repeat chevron which co-ordinates with the final pattern on the crown. This pattern can be repeated on a smaller size, where the number of rows needs to be less than that provided by pattern number 2 (the chevron).

4. The top pattern on the card (Fig. 12) is a most versatile one. It gives an illusion of shaping to the crown, and not only does it provide a many-pointed star as you look at the crown of the hat, it is a pattern used often on Norwegian-type yoked sweaters and jackets to allow for a clever and skilful colour change as soon as the pattern is finished. If you have an elongation device on your machine, employ it to lengthen the pattern into an elegant shaft of colour and pattern on the yoke of a sweater or above the hem of a dress.

There is shaping on the crown. Every other stitch is transferred to its neighbour and six rows are knitted on a tight tension in order to reduce the fullness and to draw in the centre of the crown.

The Rib Tuck Pattern

One of the most popular of all knitted hats is the head hugger with the folded back brim. The commercial varieties are mostly done in a rib tuck, fisherman's rib being a popular choice. There is no reason at all why single bed tuck cannot be employed in this pattern. The hat is of double thickness, which is produced by the stitched-up sides and end of a sausage-shaped bag being pushed in to form a hat that is very easy to wear (Fig. 13). It is important to choose a lightweight yarn. Four thicknesses of fabric could be too heavy round the forehead. The shape is very versatile however, and can easily be pulled from a head hugger into a cossack-type or pill-box hat.

Larger or smaller sizes are arrived at not only by fewer stitches on the needles but also by fewer rows. The shaping is accomplished by four methods:

1. By changing stitch pattern from normal rib to the fuller tuck rib.

main number one feed is *empty* for these four rows. A very useful piece of information that emerges is that the knitter who has no colour-changer can stripe in various colours very quickly by this method over every needle in WP. Punch a row of holes in a piece of card offcut, lock it on this row in the machine, switch to the Fair Isle setting and use colour two feed only. On the Knitmaster Electronic (SK 500) press button 1, right-hand light on, button 2, left-hand light on. The inspection button light must be on. The card can

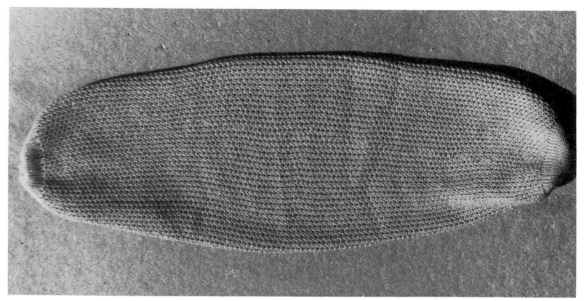

Figure 13. Rib tuck head hugger

2. By changing stitch size.

3. By the transfer and decreasing of stitches.

4. By changing from rib to stocking stitch.

The Toyota 901 single bed was the machine used to knit the ski hat. Toyota 787 owners will need to punch the card in reverse. The Passap Duomatic, long renowned for the beauty of its tuck ribs, was the obvious choice for the head hugger. The stitch can be done on the Passap either by the use of the Deco Card number 18, selector dial on 2, or by pusher selection and left arrow key down. On the Japanese punchcard machines, Knitmaster Card 2 (Fig. 14) is the same pattern. The head hugger can therefore be knitted by all machines with ribbing attachments. In any case, the card is worth punching by all non-Knitmaster punchcard owners. It has enormous stitch pattern potential. Not many machine knitters realise, for example, that this card can be used to produce single bed E O N tuck for heavy yarns, as well as single bed popcorn tuck when used in conjunction with the elongation device and stocking stitch.

To return to the head hugger, it is useful to recollect that if a single thickness hat is preferred, then a reversible pattern would be an advantage, or at least a single bed tuck pattern which looks as good on the knit side as on the purl (only a few do).

Half-fisherman's rib done on one bed (for the turned-back brim), and then reversed to the other bed for the main part of the hat, can be done on all double bed machines. The Passap alone has selection on both beds, and fully reversible fabrics, tuck ribs

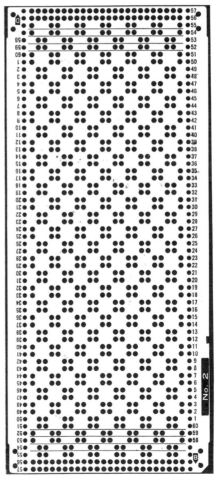

Figure 14. Knitmaster card 2

amongst them, are a popular choice for this item of clothing.

Ski Hat Pattern

Measurements
To fit head size 53.5 cm (21″). Depth including brim: 21.5 cm (8½″).

Materials
Colour 1: 50 g (2 oz) soft DK coned acrylic or equivalent.

Colour 2: 25 g (1 oz).

Tension
Fair Isle 27 sts 34 rows per 10 cm on T.9. 14.8 cm per 40 sts 17.6 cm per 60 rows.

Passap Duomatic – St S 7¼ (See Note 1).

Machine used
Toyota 901.

Main piece
Push out 146 ns. Push alt ns back to NWP. Cast on using W Y over 73 ns taking care first needle to right of O is in W P. T.7. Knit 8 rows. Knit 1 row with nylon cord. Using Col 2 in main feed, knit 16 rows. Insert P C and lock on row 1. Knit 1 row on T.8. (selecting-memorising row). Put Col 2 in feeder 2, leaving feeder 1 empty. Controls to F I. Release card RC 000 Knit 4 rows still on T.7. Change to T.8. Put Col 1 in Col 1 feed taking care not to cross yarns. Knit 12 rows. RC 16. Complete welt. RC 000. Lock card T.9. Knit 2 rows stocking stitch. Release card, knit 2

Figure 15. Ski hat

20

rows stocking stitch, then F I for 16 rows. RC 20. Lock card. Knit 2 rows stocking stitch. Release card, knit 2 rows stocking stitch, then F I for 12 rows. RC 36. Change to T.8., knit 2 rows stocking stitch as on card and 10 rows F I. RC 48. Change to Col 2 only and stocking stitch T.7. Knit 2 rows. Transfer 2nd and every alt. st to its neighbour. T.6. Knit 4 rows. T.5. Knit 4 rows. RC 58. Break off end of yarn. Thread through stitches and remove from machine.

Making up

Stitch down side seam. Remove WY from the welt. Give a light, cool press if necessary.

Notes

1. The obvious choice for ribber and for Passap Duomatic owners is the normal 1 × 1 rib welt knitted to a depth of 16 rows. There are a number of traditional chevron designs on Deco cards 46 and 48, but there is no reason why the border pattern on card 6A in the basic pack could not be repeated as often as required.

2. *J & B 840 owners.* Some of the earlier models require the NWP needles in a pattern to be removed from the bed. Check with your instruction manual and ask your dealer for advice if you wish your carriage to be modified.

3. There is no need for WY to be threaded through the yarn mast. It can be fed manually into the feed for 6–8 rows.

4. For a smaller size – 51 cm (20″) – use 4-ply yarn and T.8. instead of T.9. You will require a little less yarn of course.

Rib Tuck Head Hugger

Sizes

Small: 48 cm (19″), medium: 53.5 cm (21″), large: 58.5 cm (23″) round head.
Length (adjustable): 58.5 cm (23″), 61 cm (24″), 63.5 cm (25″).

Materials

100, 125, 150 g 4-ply acrylic/nylon on cone. (4, 5, 6 oz).

Tension

23 sts, 64 rows per 10 cm, 17.3 cm per 40 sts, 9.2 cm per 60 rows.
St S $5\frac{1}{2}$ (Passap) over 1 × 1 rib. Japanese machines with ribbers T.4/4.2.

Machine used

Passap Duomatic.

Instructions

Cast on 134, (140, 146) sts in 1 × 1 rib. Orange Strippers. Knit 10 rows 1 × 1 rib at St S 4, 10 rows at St. S $4\frac{1}{2}$ RC 000. Take pushers out of front rail and arrange 1 up, 1 down against WP needles $\frac{N}{AX}$ left arrow key down. Alternatively, use Deco card 18 SD 2. No arrow key required. Japanese machines – Knitmaster card 2 as illustrated. Controls on main bed to tuck, ribber – normal T. 4/4.2.

Graduate stitch tension up by quarters or points 20 rows at a time to St S $5\frac{1}{4}$ or T. 5/5.2.

Continue in pattern to half-way mark. Row 188, (196, 204). Adjust. Reverse stitch tension order and continue in pattern to row 376, (392, 404). Change back to 1 × 1 rib and normal knitting St S $4\frac{1}{2}$. Knit 10 rows. Transfer back bed stitches to front bed. Black strippers and stocking stitch. St S 5. Knit 1 row. Transfer every alt st to its neighbour. St S $4\frac{1}{2}$ knit 9 rows. Break off yarn. Slip off stitches onto double-eyed bodkin threaded with end of main yarn. Draw tight and fasten off.

Making up

Stitch long side seam. Turn to inside and draw in bottom end of rib to match top. Push up bottom end to inside of cap to form double thickness. Turn up brim to suit.

Notes

1. Passap Knitters are used to doing a tension swatch of 100 sts by 100 rows and reading off the required numbers from the Passap charts. The Forma, however, follows the Japanese charting device system and Passap knitters need to get used to reading per 10 cm.

Figure 16. Rib tuck head hugger

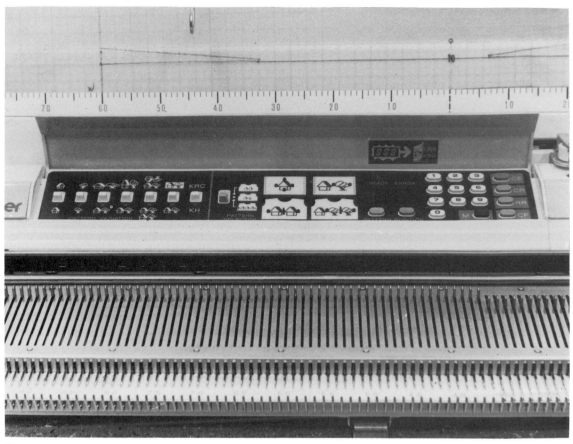

Figure 17. Brother Electroknit panel

It is very easy to do so. Go back to the Passap charts and look along the lines marked by 10 cm until you get to the reading 23 stitches and then 64 rows, or consult the chart in the last chapter of this book (Fig. 196). Look up the columns to the figures at the top. You will find that your 100 stitches – 100 rows tension swatch should measure between 43 and 44 cm in width and between 15.5 and 16 cm in length.

2. Size. The same principle as explained in the previous pattern regarding size and the use of a finer yarn applies here too. The row and stitch tension is of less importance in a pattern like this. Providing the cap fits and the shape suits and is comfortable, a stitch and a row more or less will not matter unduly.

3. This pattern provides you with the opportunity to experiment with the cards and patterns suitable for tuck rib in your pack. There is no reason why you

cannot use your colour changer and switch colours every two rows. Remember, however to begin the pattern on the left on the Japanese machines if you choose to use the colour changer.

4. J & B Electroknit owners – you can use the spaces in between existing patterns on the cards that come with your machine. Seize the opportunity to fill little spaces with your favourite small based tuck patterns. When you come to feed the information into the computer panel, be quite sure you have all the correct information with regard to position and size etc. before you attempt to programme the machine (Fig. 17). If you count wrongly, your knitting will not be correct, whether your tools be primitive or sophisticated. S K 500 owners – the pattern used for the head hugger is No. 2 on sheet one.

5. No charting device block is given for the hats. It is a simple rectangle worked out from the measurements in the pattern.

3 Gloves and mittens

If gloves represent the high summit of achievement of the knitter's art during the Middle Ages, then they also represent the perfected skills of the peasant hand knitters of England and Scotland from at least the eighteenth century onwards. There are some superb ecclesiastical gloves in museums which are of Spanish or French origin (Fig. 18), which bear witness to exquisite, painstaking craftsmanship. It is astonishing to consider that at one end of the spectrum knitting was used to produce gloves which were involved with the Sacred and Holy, and yet at the other end knitting was being practised by humble peasants to produce their rough knitted caps and coarse woollen undervests.

We do not know when glove knitting was first practised in the Yorkshire and Cumbrian dales or in the area around Sanquhar in south-west Scotland, where stocking knitting was also famous. A full description, accompanied by illustrations of Dales gloves, is to be found in *The Old Handknitters of the Dales* by Marie Hartley and Joan Ingilby (Dalesman reprint, 1978). The earliest gloves extant, some of which are in museums and textile collections in the north-west of England, are mid-nineteenth century. A knitting stick was employed and the gloves were knitted in thin wool on needles so fine that they were known as wires. The earliest gloves have a fringed cuff. All of them have the wearer's name or initials worked above the cuff (Fig. 19). More recently, small geometric Fair Isle patterns were knitted for the palm and back of the hand. In the later gloves a rib cuff welt was knitted in two colours, the knit stitch in one colour and the purl stitch in the second colour. A similar type of welt was knitted on Fair Isle sweaters in the 1920s. This is a method the machine knitter cannot emulate. It most certainly made for strength and elasticity. The fingers, like most of the glove, were knitted in the round and these had slipped stitches at the four corners to prevent wear. The machine knitter could do these if she chose.

Three of the most famous Sanquhar patterns are included in James Norbury's *Traditional Knitting Patterns* (Dover reprint, 1973). One adapted for electronic knitters and for users of the little folding machine, the Knitmaster M K 70, is included here. All three patterns are 18 stitches wide. These patterns are very interesting for another reason. The earliest Fair Isle Knitting found in the Shetlands is that on the articles found in the Gunnister burial, dated late seventeenth century. The tiny, primitive speckled check patterns bear an uncanny resemblance to the Sanquhar patterns, and indeed to the plaid patterns on the early Dales gloves. Why, one must ask, is there no resemblance to what are known as traditional Fair Isle designs? It is a great pity that hand knitting authorities have allowed themselves to be diverted by the alleged Spanish connection in Fair Isle patterns and have neglected almost completely to study a seemingly unpretentious peasant tradition, which at least has visible evidence and is featured equally in the National Museum of Antiquities in Edinburgh and in collections housed near famous national monuments like Wordsworth's Dove Cottage, Grasmere. What the hand knitter has neglected at least the machine knitter can recover before it is too late.

In defence of the Spanish connection in Fair Isle, please note that the pattern called Rose of Sharon featured in the late mediaeval gloves (Fig. 18) as well as on 'traditional' Fair Isle patterns from the 1920s onwards. (See Fig. 151.) However, though many of these romantic patterns featured earlier in em-

Figure 18. Sixteenth-century Spanish gloves. (Victoria and Albert Museum)

Figure 19. Dales gloves. The gloves on the left dated 1846, are some of the best examples of early peasant colour knitting in England. (Wordsworth and Grasmere Museum, Grasmere, Cumbria)

broidery and tapestry, no authentic colour patterns from Fair Isle knitting dated before the mid-nineteenth century are in existence to prove any theory about the Spanish connection.

Gloves, as far as many machine knitters are concerned, are the last items they would choose to knit. The reason given is that the gloves are too fiddly. The pattern in this book has been worked out with great care, so that it can be swiftly executed. The most time-consuming parts of the knitting are the fingers, but preparation by waste yarn knitting makes the process so painless that it is positively enjoyable. The pattern is one of the earliest ones in existence, from the Hunter family in Swaledale, North Yorkshire (dated around 1850 by Marie Hartley and Joan Ingilby and drawn in the *Old Handknitters of the Dales*).

The diagonal tartan plaid pattern is interesting for another reason. In 1970–1, Knitmaster marketed the 313, a semi-automatic punchcard machine, which was soon superseded by the 321. To accompany the 313 machine were sold additional packs of pre-punched cards. These cards were later discontinued.

24

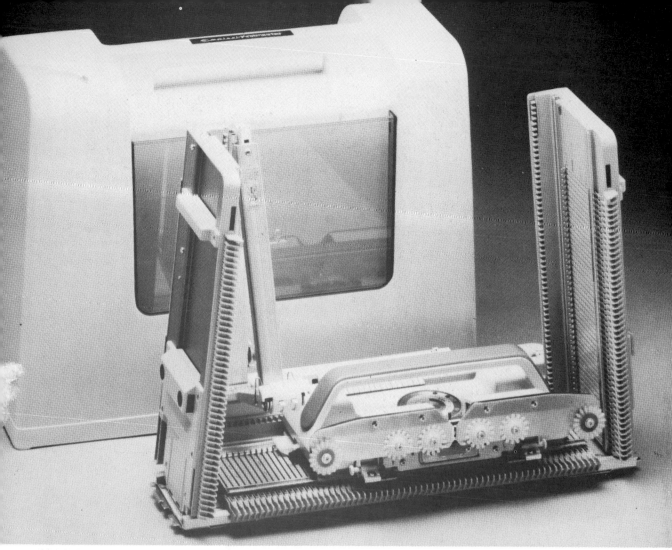

Figure 20. The Knitmaster MK 70.

Figure 21. Sanquhar pattern

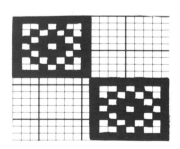

Figure 22. Sanquhar pattern (Knitmaster SK 500)

Some reappeared in paper patterns or in hardbacked books. Among those withdrawn, never to appear again, was this particular diagonal plaid (Series 26 no. 78). It is strange that the pattern (Fig. 23) should have such close traditional associations with an area the author knows so well.

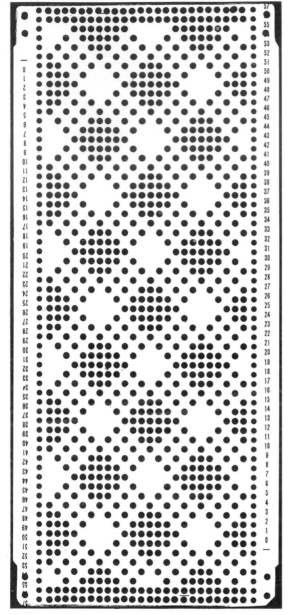

Figure 23. Punchcard for plaid pattern

Suggested Techniques

In the original Swaledale gloves, the thumb is knitted plain. If you choose to knit your name in the traditional manner, do so above the cuff before you start the plaid pattern. For the Japanese punchcard machines, turn the card over and mark the name or initials on the wrong side. Emphasise the letters by a double row at top and bottom and then punch (Fig. 24). When you turn the card back of course, you see a

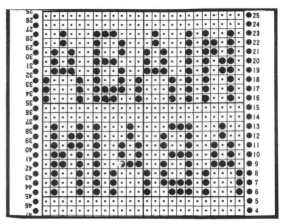

Figure 24. Punched name on card off-cut. Write and punch the name on the wrong side (top). Turn over (bottom) and insert in the machine

mirror image, which will come out the right way in the knitting. Passap Duomatic owners can write the name and punch it on the right side of the Deco card. On the Passap, the front bed is the dominant bed and the card moves upwards into the Deco reader. There is no mirror image problem.

The cuff is knitted in the usual 1 × 1 rib or 2 × 1 single bed welt, but there is no reason why you should not fringe the cuffs in the traditional nineteenth-century manner. The thumb, unlike the handknitted version, is added on afterwards by an unusual graft-knitting process that has many creative possibilities in other contexts. This method means that the Fair Isle portion can be knitted very fast indeed. The fingers, of course, are plain. If you have a ribbing attachment or a double bed machine, the quickest way to knit the fingers and the top part of the thumb is by circular knitting. You will then eliminate time-consuming seams. Passap knitters should choose a small-based Fair Isle or single bed BX (slip) pattern.

The mittens pattern is included for those who do not yet wish to tackle a glove pattern, though it is hoped they will soon be persuaded to do so. Mittens are so easy and are such a delightful accompaniment to hats that they have been made to match as nearly as possible. There are various ways to knit them. In this pattern, the multiple finger-shaping is 'turned' like the heel of a sock and the raw edges below the waste yarn grafted together (Fig. 25). The thumb opening is by the waste yarn buttonhole method and is the machine knitters' quick answer to complicated increasing across the palm. Let it be said, however, that the graft knitted thumbs on the gloves allow for more ease. They may look too long but the extra length is illusion. They fit where they touch, with perfection.

Figure 25. Fair Isle hat and mittens

Lady's Gloves

Size
To fit average-to-large hand. Length of fingers adjustable. Overall length: $25\frac{1}{2}$ cm ($10\frac{1}{4}''$). Girth of palm above thumb: 17 cm ($7''$).

Materials
Colour 1: 35 g (2 oz) 3-ply wool.

Colour 2: 20 g (1 oz).

Pattern
Diagonal plaid punchcard as illustrated, or equivalent small-based pattern for single bed Fair Isle.

Tension
Stocking stitch 32 sts 48 rows per 10 cm.

12.5 cm per 40 sts, 12.5 cm per 60 rows. T.4.2 (Passap St S $4\frac{3}{4}$).

Fair Isle – 33 sts 46 rows per 10 cm.

18.1 cm per 40 sts, 12.9 cm per 60 rows. T.5.2. (Passap $5\frac{1}{2}$).

Machine used
J & B 840.

Figure 26. Fair Isle gloves

Right and left glove
Cast on 56 sts. Knit 30 rows in 1 × 1 rib T. $\frac{1}{4}$. Single bed machines, knit 30 rows, 1 fold row, 30 rows in 2 × 1 mock welt. T.2.1. Change to stocking stitch and Fair Isle set up. Inc. 1 stitch at each end. T.5.2. Arrange for F I R C 000. Knit 38 rows in pattern. Dec

27

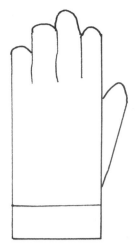

Figure 27. Glove. Length: 25 cm (10½ in), girth 17 cm (7 in)

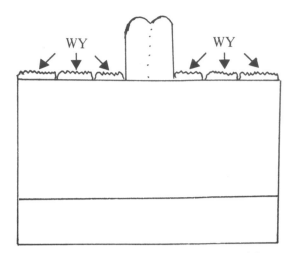

Figure 28. Glove opened out, after the knitting of the little finger. The waste yarn holding the stitches for the other fingers is shown

1 stitch at beg of next 2 rows to 56 sts. RC 40. Carr at right.

Break off Col 1 and 2. Thread up WY. Carr to hold and to stocking stitch.

Push all ns except 7 at right to HP (Passap BX and pushers). Knit 6 rows over these 7 ns. Break yarn and release from machine. Push empty ns to NWP * Push next 7 ns nearest carr back into UWP (WP pushers on Passap). Knit 6 rows in WY and release from machine. Break yarn and push empty ns to NWP **.

Repeat from * to ** once more. Take carr to left of bed and repeat from * to ** 3 more times. There are 6 times 7 sts on WY released from machine. Take carr to right and continue as follows.

Fourth (little) Finger

(Knitted on centre 14 sts). Push ns back to UWP. RC 000. T.4.2. Inc f f with 2 eyed tool 1 stitch at each end (16 sts) RC 000. Knit in stocking st 30 rows. Adjust length.

Shape top

Transfer every alt st to its neighbour. T.2.2. Knit 2 rows. Break end of yarn. Take sts off onto yarn. Draw up and use end for stitching side seam of finger.

Third finger

Pick up 7 sts nearest to completed finger on right below WY. Remove WY. Inc 1 stitch f f each end. Pick up 7 stitches nearest to completed finger on left leaving room to inc 1 stitch f f each end. Remove WY (18 sts in all). RC 000. Knit 34 rows. Adjust. Top as for little finger.

Second finger

Pick up sts as for third finger. RC 000. Knit 38 rows. Adjust. Top as for little finger.

Index finger

Pick up sts as for third finger. RC 000. Knit 34 rows. Adjust. Top as for little finger.

Thumb

Cast on by hand 1 stitch. Knit 1 row by hand. T.4.2. RC 000. Turn glove inside out. Fold over welt towards the machine. Inc. 1 stitch at beg of next and foll rows by hitching an edge loop of main piece onto empty needle, one from each side of glove. * Knit 2 rows. Inc 1 stitch as above at beg. of next 2 rows. 9 times altog. RC 36 (21 sts) Knit 30 rows straight. Adjust length. RC 66. Shape top as for little finger.

Making Up

Stitch all seams. Overcast on inside of graft-knitted thumb, if necessary. Press according to yarn.

Notes

1. Knit these gloves once and you will soon realise how adaptable the pattern is. Indeed, you could use tuck or slip patterns providing you make slight adjustments of tension. Notice the difference in tension between stocking stitch and this particular Fair Isle. Every Fair Isle pattern produces a slightly different tension. It depends equally on the float span and on the pull of the fabric lengthways. The general rule is that Fair Isle has a stitch or two more per 10 cm than stocking stitch and a row or two less. If you are a hand knitter as well as a machine knitter, you will notice that you achieve about 4 rows less per 10 cm with a pair of needles knitting stocking stitch than you do on the machine.

For this glove pattern you can reduce the stitches

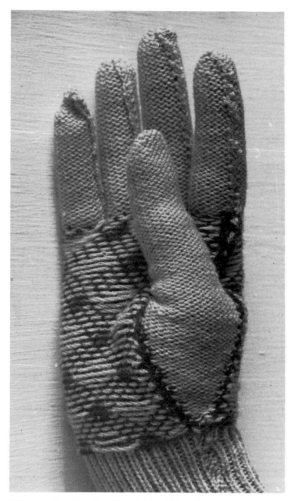

Fig. 29. Inside of grafted knitted thumb

(b) the tilt of the ribber tends to tighten a stitch as it is formed. Always test a ribber pattern for construction before you proceed.

3. The double eyed bodkin is useful for the single bed knitter. Break the yarn at the top of the glove fingers. Thread the end through one eye of the double-eyed bodkin and use the other to take off the stitches to be drawn up. Stitch the side seams with the bodkin. Its blunt head is kind to stitches and it

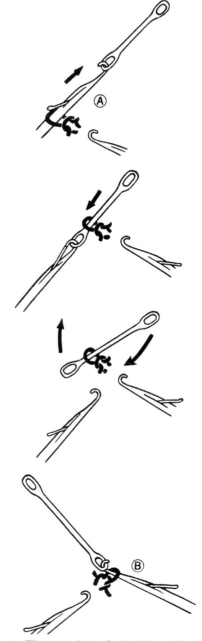

Figure 30. The operations of a double-eyed bodkin

proportionately for smaller sizes, making quite sure that you have made allowances for children's fingers, which can be about the same girth as those of an average adult. You will not need the same length of course. Feel free to increase the number of stitches at the top of the palm to cope with the circumference of the fingers.

2. *Circular knitting and the ribbing attachment.* The number of stitches involved in knitting the fingers and thumb is so small that you will not require to hang the ribber weights or even insert the comb. When you have distributed the stitches evenly between main bed and ribber, weave a fine knitting needle in and out of the glove fabric and suspend a small weight. Put the tension to 5 on the ribber. It often needs to be higher than the main bed because:

(a) the needles are smaller and have a shorter range of withdrawal to form a stitch;

does not split the yarn in the stitching up process. The double-eyed bodkin is included in the equipment of every double bed machine and ribbing attachment. It is essential you learn how to use it for the transfer of stitches from one bed to the other. Use it also to take off stitches for the centre neck onto waste yarn. The bodkin costs only a few pence to buy, but it is well worth its weight in gold (Fig. 30).

4. *Tip*. Have a pair of small sharp scissors near the machine to snip any tangled ends and avoid irritation.

5. Any row and stitch tension worked out for a swatch of 40 sts and 60 rows, which has a ratio of 2 to 3, will work out as a square. 32 sts and 48 rows make a square, the sides of which measure 12.5 cm. The tension squares of either 100 sts and 100 rows or 40 sts and 60 rows are worked out as a mathematical formula. In stocking stitch, two common stitch and row ratios are 2 to 3 and 3 to 4. Most stocking stitch tensions achieve a ratio near one of those two. Tuck stitch is very different. With fewer stitches and more rows per 10 cm, the ratio is more like 1 to 2 or 1 to 3. In slip stitch, the stitches approximate to Fair Isle and the row situation is comparable to tuck. Knit-

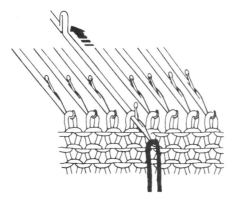

Figure 31. How to mark a stitch

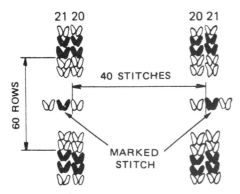

Figure 32. Marking a 40 stitch–60 row swatch

weave comes between stocking stitch and tuck. Dyes and yarn type affect tension and a tension swatch should always be knitted. Charting device owners are in the best position of all.

Mittens

Size
To fit an average hand. Overall length: 23 cm (9″). Girth above thumb: 19 cm ($7\frac{1}{2}$″).

Materials
Colour 1: 25 g (1 oz) soft coned DK acrylic.
Colour 2: 25 g (1 oz).

Tension
Fair Isle 27 sts 34 rows per 10 cm on T.9.
14.8 cm per 40 sts 17.7 cm per 60 rows.
Passap Duomatic St S $7\frac{1}{4}$ (for small based F I).

Machine used
Toyota 901.

Right Mitten
Push out 45 ns to WP. Take back to NWP every alt n. 23 sts left in WP. Knit 16 rows in T.7. fold row on T.9. 16 rows on T.7. Complete single bed welt. RC 33.

Double bed welt. Knit 16 rows 1 × 1 rib T.$\frac{4}{5}$.

Change to stocking st and T.8. Inc 1 stitch f f at right edge (46 sts). RC 000 knit 4 rows. Select for FI on row 4. Change to T.9. Inc 1 stitch f f at beg of next 2 rows and every 2nd and 3rd row 4 times altog RC 15. (54 sts). Knit 1 row to complete 8 stitch base chevron. Carr at right. At extreme left of knitting and using a piece of contrast yarn, knit off 9 sts (WY buttonhole method) by hand, for thumb opening.

Roll back card to beg of pattern and lock. Change to stocking st. Knit 2 rows, selecting memorizing pattern on second row. Release card and repeat pattern once more. Knit 2 rows and change to final pattern on card. Knit 10 rows in F I. Change to stocking st and knit 1 row to left (RC 43). Set carr to hold. Push out 23 sts. right of O to HP break off MY. Knit 6 rows of WY over 23 ns at left in WP. Release from machine. Take carr to right. Thread in MY RC 000. Push back all but extreme left needle (next to O) back to UWP. Knit the row. Cont to push out 1 needle opp carr to HP, 16 rows in all. Push back 1 needle opp carr to UWP on next 16 rows (RC 32), remembering to wrap needle next to WP needles to prevent a hole. Knit 6 rows in WY and release from machine.

Figure 33. Fair Isle mittens

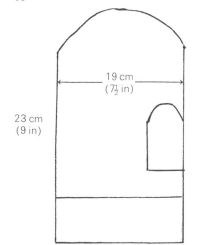

19 cm
(7½ in)

23 cm
(9 in)

Figure 34. The mittens – essential measurements

Left Mitten

As right mitten, but knit one extra row after welt to bring carr to left, and read left for right. Thumb opening on right on row 17.

Thumb

Remove waste yarn and pick up 20 sts and loops from opened out raw edge (top and bottom), making sure to pick up 2 at the turn to prevent holes. Knit 19 rows on T.8. Transfer every alt st to its neighbour. Knit 1 row T.4, break yarn and draw end through sts on needles. Release from machine.

Making up

Graft sts at top. Remove WY. Stitch side seams and thumbs. A light cool press can be given, if necessary.

Notes

1. There is a question of design involved here with

regard to the size, shape and use of the mittens. The larger chevron would have been out of place on the mittens and the large floats a nuisance.

2. You can organise the WY rows at the beginning so that you have no need to knit an extra row in the MY for the left mitten. Double bed and ribber owners need only to knit an extra bound off, cast on circular row and start, then count for the rib at the left.

3. *Tip for the WY buttonhole method thumb.* Take a fine knitting needle and as you pull out the WY slip the stitches and loops they hold on to the knitting needle. At the turn, twist the connecting strands to form 2 loops and then continue to pick up until you have a total of 20 to replace on the machine.

4. *How else could you knit these mittens?*
(a) You could divide the sts by half (23 sts). Knit the front. Turn the finger ends in the manner of a heel and knit the back. The thumb would be in the same place and by the same method. There would be 2 long side seams, but the great advantage would be that you could choose to have a different pattern for the palm and the back of the hand.

(b) Double bed and ribber owners could knit the pattern circular. With the exception of Passap Duomatic owners, patterning, other than stripes, would not be possible. The thumb method would be similar, but the shaping at the top of the hand would have to be organised so that one stitch on each bed would be decreased fully fashioned on each circular row, first at the right and then at the left. (8 × 2 sts at each side.)

5. *Practise decreasing and increasing fully fashioned* (Figs 35 and 36). There are instructions and diagrams in every instruction book. Fully-fashioned increasing is the more difficult of the two. Make quite sure you have lifted the head-loop of the stitch below (either to the left or right) and not just the strand which separated the stitches. You can use either the two-eyed or the three-eyed transfer tool. Fully-fashioned increasing and decreasing ensures that you have smooth edges for the seam.

6. *The selecting-memorising row.* When you are selecting patterns at random from various positions on the card, you have to be adept at using the pattern memory or selection system of your machine. You cannot be adept until you understand how it works. There are four systems involved in the most popular machines currently available.

(a) *The Knitmaster Card Memory.* This is the longest established of the punchcard systems. The card can be inserted at any time during the rib, or before the pattern is due to take place. It can be locked and forgotten until you are ready to pattern

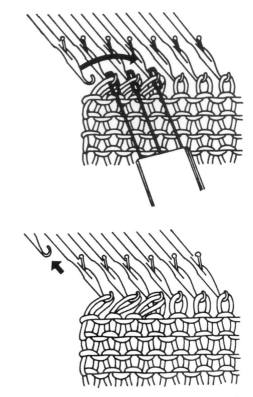

Figure 35. Fully-fashioned decreasing using the three-eyed transfer tool

knit. Switch the cams to the pattern required, release the card and begin. Pattern knitting takes place with all needles at B position. Should you have forgotten to insert the card until the pattern row is the next to knit, remove the yarn, disconnect the row counter, insert the card, lock on the correct row, set the carriage to free move slip (side levers forward) and take it across the bed. Reset the carriage, insert the yarn, release the card and away you go. N.B. The newest models have a release catch for a quicker free move slip (Fig. 37).

(b) *The J & B and Toyota 901 machines.* The main differences between these and the Knitmaster system is that the selection mechanism is in the bed and not in the carriage. The mechanism works in harmony with the punchcard and directs the needle to B position (for normal, tuck or slip), and D position for Fair Isle and lace. In knitweave the weaving yarn is usually laid in front of the D position needles and trapped between the old stitch and the new yarn on a B position needle, but this is not always so and knitweave patterns are worth studying for the interesting variations they can achieve.

When the carriage is switched to pattern, it immediately gears into the system. Selected needles are

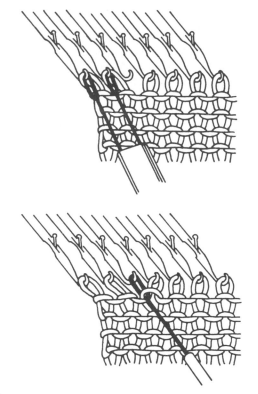

Figure 36. Fully-fashioned increasing using the two-eyed transfer tool

Figure 37. Knitmaster 360 (Knitmaster)

brought to D position. Allowance must be made for this row in the knitting. You can switch to pattern on the last plain row. Selection is made as you knit the row and you are ready to pattern knit. If you have forgotten to select, then remove the yarn, disengage the row counter and charting device trip, switch the carriage to plain knitting and its cams to part, slip or empty. Take the carriage to the opposite end in a free move. Now switch to pattern, still keeping the cams on part, slip or empty. Take the carriage back to its original position. Selection is made and you are ready to set all systems in motion again and begin to pattern knit. All you need is to learn a drill (Fig. 38).

N.B. If you free move slip when some needles are already selected to D position, the D position needles will drop their stitches. Push any D position needles back to B position and then select.

(c) *The Electronic Systems.* These follow the needle position principles as above according to the make of machine. Direction of needles is controlled by electronic means, a silicon chip or by an electro-mechanical card-scanning process (Superba).

N.B. The J & B Electroknit 910 must have all data programmed into its computer panel for each pattern you wish to select. Again, it's a drill to learn and an interesting one. The SK 500 is similar. The electronic machines can be so fascinating that you can treat them like games and forget they are there to knit!

(d) *The Passap Deco* (Fig. 40). This is probably nearest to the Knitmaster System. The advantage

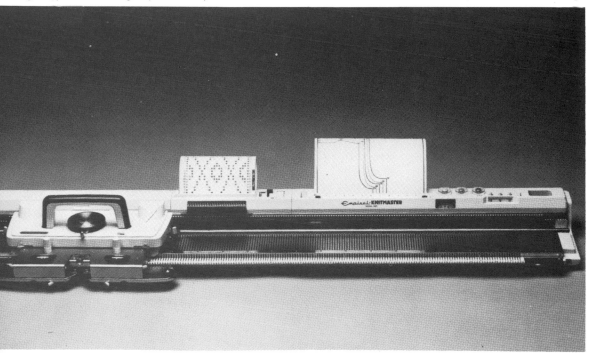

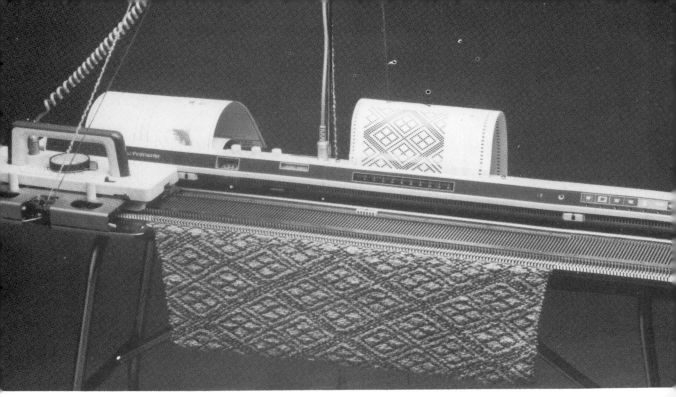

Figure 39. The Knitmaster SK 500 (Electronic)
(Knitmaster)

Figure 38. Brother 830 (Jones & Brother)

Figure 40. Passap Selector (Bogod & Co.)

here is that the selector can be unclipped from the carriage and taken over the pushers to memorise the position of the feelers.

Tips for all punchcard machines

Always mark with a pencil on the punchcard where the first row of pattern begins, 5 rows up (Knitmaster), 7 rows up (J & B, Toyota, Passap) or 4 rows up

(Singer, Juki). The punchcard is carried by the Juki cambox, but its needle selection system is similar to both the Brother and Toyota machines.

The electronic machines move the card down automatically to the point for selection, as soon as you programme the pattern and turn the card to the set line.

4 Jerseys and guernseys

One of the earliest written references to the knitted over-garment of the sailor is of William the Silent donning the traditional garb to identify himself with his seafaring nation and with the sufferings of the Dutch people under the Spanish oppressor in the sixteenth century. There is strong evidence to suggest a fisher tradition of jersey- and guernsey-wearing from the north of Scotland right down the eastern seaboard of England, to the Channel Islands and across again to Cornwall. Why the fisher knitting ended here is a mystery. Perhaps it has something to do with the journey's end of the shoals of herring. Be that as it may, Wales and the north-west of England have no tradition of fisher knitting.

Since the 1930s it has been fashionable to include Aran knitting with fisher knitting and to claim that the beautiful sculpturesque patterns are on sweaters worn by the human characters in the ninth century *Book of Kells*. No one seems to be able to explain, however, why the animals and letters are as be-knotted and be-patterned as the people in that famous Celtic manuscript. The documentary evidence, given in full in 'The History of Knitted Fashion' in my *Second Resource Book for Machine Knitters*, points to twentieth century beginnings. Aran knitting nevertheless remains some of the most mysterious and the most beautiful in the world.

There is a distinction between a jersey and a guernsey. Traditionally, jerseys were made of finer wool and less patterned than the heavier guernsey (or gansey). In the Yorkshire Dales, 'pop' jackets and 'spotted frocks' were knitted from the late-eighteenth century onwards on hand frames as well as by hand knitters. We have written evidence, but no actual garments. Hand frames in the east Midlands were turning out pieces for fashionable waistcoats

and jackets for men earlier than this. Frocks and shirts were terms used in Cornwall to describe handknitted overgarments. So far these items refer mostly to garments worn by sailors and country people. In the 1890s, Lily Langtry, the actress friend of Edward, Prince of Wales, achieved the distinction of being the first fashionable woman to dare to wear in public a knitted outer garment, a jersey from her native Channel Islands. It caused more than a sensation, it was an outrage.

Thirty years on, after the trauma of the First World War, when women were demanding sartorial recognition for their new status, Chanel remembered Lily Langtry. Industrial sources confirm that Chanel was the French designer who went to the east Midlands and bought some fine cashmere, silk and wool men's undershirts from an English firm making them on hand frames. Chanel remodelled the garments and gave them touches and trimmings which elevated the knitted (machine-made) outer garment to the top rank of fashion.

The disadvantages of the hand frame were that it could not knit patterned fabric in the round in the manner of the handknitter or indeed, like the Passap Duomatic machine of today. Unlike all modern domestic machines, the frame had no holding cam levers and fabric could not be shaped automatically, without bulk, by holding position needles. Moreover, Chanel realised that the dropped shoulder line, non-shaped garment of the peasant and the sailor was not always acceptable to the lady of fashion. Dressmaking principles were applied to jersey fabric. The armhole was carved out either by cut and sew or by fully fashioned shaping, and the fitted sleeve 'jumper', as Chanel called it, was born. Though indeed the drop shoulder line shape was

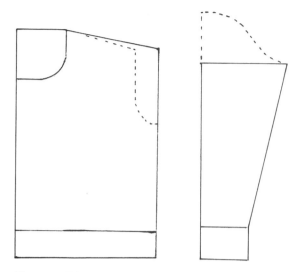

never forgotten, the fitted sleeve style was to become the essential and the most versatile of all. It is interesting that the modern machine knitter finds it easier to develop the drop shoulder block for the charting device from the fitted sleeve shape. The original norm is now one of several modified shapes developed from the basic fitted sleeve pattern (Fig. 41).

Recently, in the so-called ethnic revival, the dropped shoulder line top has become very popular. It is easy to make (especially in complicated stitch patterns) and easy to wear. The lore of the jersey and guernsey has leapt to the forefront of every knitting book and the plain garter trimmed guernsey is a popular choice for hand and machine knitters alike, who choose to knit the garment in its earliest, basic form.

Figure 41. The development of the dropped shoulder line from the fitted sleeve block

Figure 42. Traditional Staithes (Yorkshire) handknit gansey

In the late 1930s or early 1940s a now forgotten knitting authority, Jane Koster, made a memorable journey by foot down the north-east coast of England from Seahouses to Hull, collecting knitting patterns as she went. She told the following story in a lecture delivered to the Wool Society on 22 January 1957. In Whitby, Jane Koster asked why the knitters put cables onto the unusual saddle shoulders of their ganseys, and was told that, 'a long time ago', there was a plague of snakes in Yorkshire. St Brigid came over from Ireland and looked at the snakes. Some went into the rocks and became ammonites and the others the knitters put onto the shoulders of their ganseys. Since Brigid is the Christianized name for Brigantia, the Celtic fire and water goddess, whose statue stands in the Roman undercroft of York Minster, this knitting story stirs a folk memory as deep and as ancient as any (Fig. 42).

In a second-hand book shop, some four years ago, I bought for a few pence a tattered volume called *Modern Knitting Illustrated* by Jane Koster and Margaret Murray and published by Odhams in 1945. In the pattern collection is a dropped shoulder line man's jersey, knitted in the round, with cables going partway up the chest and right across the unusual saddle shoulders. It is that garment which gave the inspiration for the machine-knit jersey in this book.

The Jersey-Gansey-Shape

There is more yet to interest the student of knitted garment shapes. Dropped shoulder lines are popular and saddle shoulders not uncommon, especially on commercial garments. It is unusual, however, to have the two features together in one garment.

Unlike the jersey hand knitter, the machine knitter does not do the bulk of the garment in the round. The back, front and sleeves are knitted separately and the epaulettes and sleeve-head side grafted or mattress-stitched to the back and front. This takes time, but it is worth it for a perfect finish (Fig. 43). For speed, however, cast off instead of holding on WY and stitch or link the pieces together. One size only is given as space is limited. The abbreviations are not used consistently, to enable those who wish to study the pattern for the techniques to move swiftly through the reading (Fig. 44).

It is of value to explain how the pattern was designed. As always, the charting device was used. The basic pattern was a dropped shoulder line block with a conventional round neck (evolved from a fitted sleeve block in my *Second Resource Book for Machine Knitters*). Any suitable pattern can be chosen. The dotted outline in Fig. 45 is the original. The most

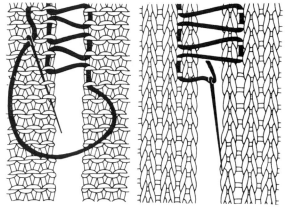

Figure 43. Mattress stitch, at edge (left) and one stitch in (right)

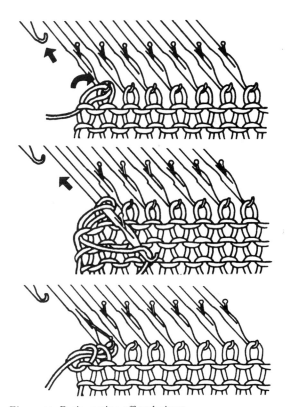

Figure 44. Basic casting off technique

difficult part of the design is the epaulette forming the saddle. Its width is 7.5 cm, so from E to Q is 3.75 cm. The original line G R was retained in order to provide a high neck. To be consistent, you can drop it 0.75 cm to allow A S to be 3.75 cm instead of 3 cm. There is flexibility here. Certainly, on larger sizes the neckline should be deeper.

S T = G R and is, of course, half A F. T Q

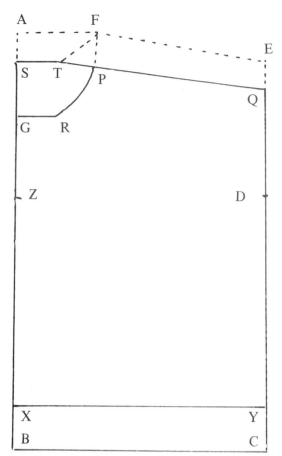

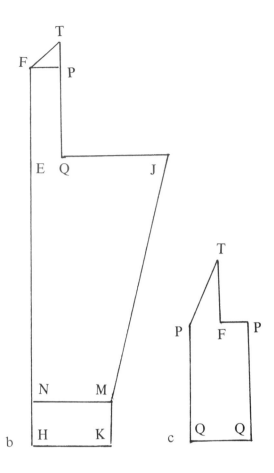

Figure 45(a) & (b). The jersey-gansey shape developed from the dropped shoulder-line block.

SB	= 60 cm (24 in)		FH	= 64 cm (25¼ in)
BC	= 25.5 cm (10 in)		FE	= 18 cm (7 in)
ST	= 4 cm (1½ in)		FP	= 4 cm (1½ in)
TQ	= 21.5 cm (8½ in)		TP	= 3.25 cm (1¼ in)
TP	= 3.5 cm (1½ in)		QJ	= 18.5 cm (7¼ in)
QD	= 18 cm (7 in)		NH	= 7 cm (2¾ in)
XB	= 7 cm (2¾ in)		JM	= 40 cm (15¾ in)

Figure 45(c). The opened-out epaulette. The shaping FP is done at one side of the epaulette, or saddle, FT at the other. These shapings are reversed for the second sleeve. FP = front, FT = back

represents the back shoulder seam and the back seam of the epaulette. P Q similarly represents the front seam. As it stands, the curved edge of the epaulette and its seams fit and match to perfection. The neckband, too, is most comfortable.

On the epaulette, the lines F T P are identical with those on the main block. F P represents a group of stitches which must be cast off or held on WY on one side for the first sleeve and on the other side for the second. You should now be equipped to draw a block for your own size, but read the pattern and its notes first.

Unisex Jersey (Double Bed Machines)

Size
To fit 96.5 cm (38 in) chest. Measurements as shown Fig. 45.

Materials
500 g of 3 × $\frac{2}{16}$ English crossbred wool, or equivalent 4-ply.

Tension
30 sts, 41 rows per 10 cm, 13.3 cm per 40 sts and 14.7 cm per 60 rows on the Passap Duomatic. St S 6. T.6 Japanese machines (stocking stitch).

Machine used
Passap Duomatic 80. (Orange strippers for rib. Black strippers for stocking stitch.) Passap instructions are first. See Note 1.

Back
Push up on main bed 150 ns. Take back the 3rd needle. Push up on 2nd bed or ribber needles to form

Figure 46. Unisex cabled jersey

arrangement for 2 : 1 industrial rib. Handle down (half pitch 5). Follow procedure shown in Fig. 47.

Ensure that the main bed needles are the outsiders. Rack the bed one full turn to the right for the cast on row. St S $3\frac{1}{2}$ T$\frac{3}{3}$.

Knit 2 CX (circular) rows. Rack the bed back to its original position. Arrange for rib knitting St S 5, T$\frac{3}{4}$. Passap: knit 1 row to right. RC 000. Lock – carr at right. Rib 24 rows. Change to stocking stitch. St S 6, T 6. Knit 124 rows (adjust). Tie edge stitch at each side with a piece of WY to mark beg of armhole. RC 000. Arrange for side cables. Starting from right have 4 sts on main bed, 2 sts on RB, 6 sts on MB, 2 sts on RB, 6 sts on MB, 2 sts on RB. Do left side the same but read left for right. Put handle up (full pitch) St S $\frac{6\frac{1}{2}}{6}$, T $\frac{6}{6.2}$.

Knit 8 rows. Cable 3 over 3 ns in each group of 6, letting dominant hand hold 3 sts while the second hand crosses over and deposits the other 3 sts onto the needles which were emptied first.

Continue in pattern and knit to row 78. Lock carr at right. Arrange lock and MB for BX and pushers (holding position). Put pushers into RP (HP) against 11, 11, 10, 10, 10, 10, ns opposite lock – carr on next 12 rows. Each figure represents 2 rows. (62 sts held for each shoulder, 6 rows each side). Knit 6 rows WY over 26 sts in centre. Release, knit 6 rows WY over 62 sts held at extreme left by putting pushers into WP (UWP). Do same for sts at right.

Front

Knit as for back to row 74 above armhole. Take off onto WY 13 sts either side of O (26 sts in middle).

Front neck

Knit 1 row. Cast off 3 sts at beg of next and following alt row. Knit 1 row. Row 78, shoulder shaping begins. Lock – carr as for back. BX and pushers (holding position). Put pushers into RP (HP) against.

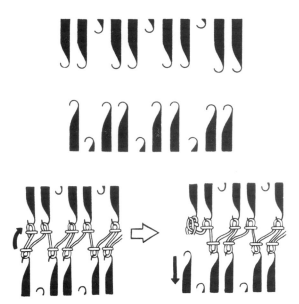

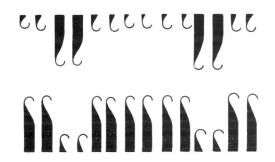

Figure 47. The 2 × 1 industrial rib; needle arrangements

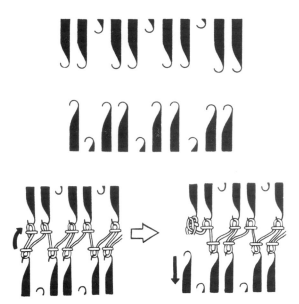

Figure 48. Cable set-up for the Passap

11, 11, 10, 10, 10, ns opposite lock – carr on next 10 rows. Each figure represents 2 rows. (52 sts held for each shoulder. 5 rows each side). Continue shaping at neck.

Side: cast off 2 sts at beg of next and foll alt row. Knit 1 row. Dec 1 stitch at beg of next and every alt row 3 times altog. Complete as for back.

Right sleeve

Push up 72 ns on MB. Arrange for 2:1 industrial rib as for back. St S 5 T$\frac{3}{4}$. Knit 24 rows. RC 000. Change to stocking stitch. St S 6, T 6. Inc 1 stitch at each end of every 5th row 18 times. Inc 1 stitch at each end of every 4th row 15 times (138 sts). Row 150. Knit straight to Row 156. Adjust. Use BX and pushers (HP). Scrap off in WY 57 sts to right of centre 24 sts, then 57 sts at left of centre 24 sts. Release these 2

groups of 57 sts from the machine. Cont on rem 24 sts in centre.

Epaulette

Inc 1 stitch at each side of 24 sts = 26 sts. Arrange cables as for back, but begin and end with 4 sts. RC 000.

Cable every 8th row as for back. At row 74 (75 on second sleeve) take off 12 sts opp lock-carr onto double-eyed bodkin threaded with WY. Tie and leave. Cont on 14 sts. Knit 1 row lock-carr at left. Cast off 3 sts at beg of next row. Knit 1 row. Cast off 2 sts at beg of next and foll alt rows 3 times altog. Knit 1 row. Dec 1 stitch at beg of next and every alt row 3 times. Cast off rem 2 sts.

Left sleeve

As for right. Follow alt instructions where indicated and read left for right (Fig. 49).

Neckband

Graft or sew left back and front to left epaulette. Graft front right to front of right epaulette, leaving right back open. Remove WY. Open beds and slip up between them the stitched-together garment pieces, right side facing. Pick up 133 sts evenly all round neck edge and place on back bed needles. Remove WY. Inc 1 stitch at each end (135 sts). Close beds, handle up (full pitch). Knit 1 row stocking stitch on MT. Transfer 3rd and every foll 3rd stitch to the appropriate empty needle on the opp bed. Weights for Japanese machines and Superba-Singer. RC 000 St S$\frac{5}{4}$ knit 6 rows. St S $\frac{4\frac{3}{4}}{3\frac{3}{4}}$ knit 6 rows. St S $\frac{4\frac{1}{2}}{3\frac{1}{2}}$ knit 6 rows. Knit 1 fold row on St S$\frac{6}{5}$. Reverse tensions for next 18 rows. (Japanese machines: begin rib tension one point higher than for welt). RC 37. Lock-carr at right. Transfer all sts to back bed. Change to st st and knit 2 rows on MT. Change to WY and knit 6 rows. Release from machine.

Making up

Close rem shoulder. Continue stitching up the seam of the neckband. Fold over neckband. Pin into place and backstitch through sts of first row of MY above WY. Remove WY. Graft or stitch sides of sleeve head between marked points of back and front. Remove WY. Stitch sleeve seams and ribs. Press all except cable and ribs.

Notes

1. The Passap Duomatic first appeared on the market in 1961 and its considerable pattern literature is of real interest to machine knitters who like to dip

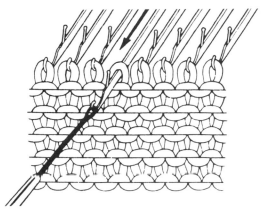

Figure 49. Basic tool-holding technique

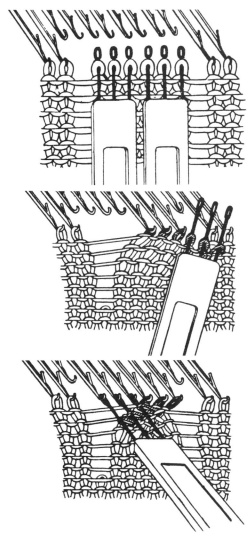

Figure 50. Cabling procedure for single bed Japanese machines

into past culture for new ideas. Learning to decipher for the Japanese machines (and vice versa) is well worth the effort. This pattern is written bilingually to provide a way forward.

The dominant bed on the Passap is the front bed, therefore the needle arrangement should be reversed for Japanese and Superba machines. Similarly, the right sleeve will be the left sleeve on the Japanese and Superba machines (Figs 50 and 51).

2. *The 2:1 Industrial rib*. This causes unnecessary confusion. You need to understand that you must rack the bed to make a zigzag row and one that will form stitches. Then you must rack back again for the rib. Additional needles put up to make the zigzag row knit at the edges can be drawn back to NWP and their stitches transferred as soon as the zigzag row is complete. The pair of needle outsiders on the main bed are there to ensure that the seams are matched. Equally, you can choose to have them on the ribber or second bed. The point at issue is that the row must begin and end with a pair.

3 *The Neckband*. The 2:1 industrial rib is suitable only for a neckband which is applied separately, usually finished with tubular rows and put on cut and sew necklines. Picking up stitches on the neckline provides a quicker method and this one is a well-tried favourite. The 2:1 industrial rib will not do, however, as it provides more stitches than the total complement round the neckline. The 2:1 rib on a full pitch setting does provide a match of stitch for stitch, and simulates the industrial rib so well that it is difficult to tell the difference.

N.B. The Passap back bed is used as the main bed for the neckband.

4. Confident handling of the tools is the key to machine-knitting success, as in any handicraft. The machine knitter must master her or his tools sufficiently to enjoy using them. Experienced dealers often give potential customers plenty of practice with transfer and work tools before selling the machine. Nothing reveals the extent of the machine knitter's skill more than the ability to make cables. A good springy yarn is essential and this one is an industrial crossbred wool on cone. The original wool in the hand knitting pattern was crossbred 4-ply knitted on a fairly tight tension to give a firm fabric. Passap knitters will require a second black transfer tool.

When cabling, the machine knitter needs to hold her transfer tools correctly. If the tools are tilted the wrong way or held with a shaky hand, the stitches will drop. The latches must be flicked open with the tool-head before the stitches can be deposited. In the series of diagrams printed here (Fig. 50) only one

Figure 51. The cabled shoulders of the machine-knitted jersey

stitch on either side of the cable is transferred out of action, but in the jersey pattern there are two. As the pattern is written for double bed owners these pairs of stitches go on the second bed. The ribber, however, is not designed to knit back large groups of stitches on the main bed on the stocking stitch setting. To overcome this problem, push out to HP (and set the cam levers to knit back) one needle in twenty or so across the bed. Do this on every row to ensure perfect knitting (Figs 52 and 53).

Single bed knitters can hold the two stitches on small safety pins. Crochet the stitches up at intervals using the work or latchet tool. This procedure will make two purl stitches to flank the cable on either side.

In the pattern, the tension balance has been carefully worked out and tried. Sometimes you may find that the carriage won't knit the row after the crossover of stitches. The stitches are held taut and cannot be drawn back by the cams to form the next row. There are two alternatives to try:

(a) On the Japanese machines and Superba push out the cabling needles to HP. Loosen the stitch tension a point and set the cams to knit the needles back.

(b) On the Passap and on all double bed machines (ribbers included) put up on the second bed on the row before the crossover 2 needles with a space of 2 between them, opposite each group of 6 cabling needles. Put the handle down (racking handle to half pitch). Knit the row and the 2 extra needles per cable set up will have collected loops which can be eased into the crossover. Remember to push the extra needles back to NWP and put the handle up (return the bed to full pitch).

Passap owners may need to practise cables more than any other machine knitter and this jersey was done on the Passap, so that every possible difficulty could be explored. As the dominant bed is the front bed, the tools cannot be tilted upright as on the Japanese machines and the Superba, although Passap owners could take the easy way out and use the back bed as the main one. In this pattern, no specific instruction has been given as to the direction of the

42

Figure 52. J & B 840 with ribber. (Jones & Brother)

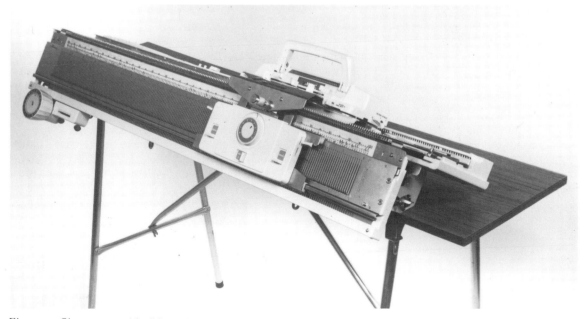

Figure 53. Singer 2500 with ribber. (Singer U.K.)

Figure 54. Lady's Lace top (Chapter 7), sleeveless Fair Isle waistcoat (Chapter 8) and traditional jersey

cable twist so let the dominant hand be the leader. Right-handed knitters will take off 3 stitches first with the right hand and hold them while the left hand takes off the second batch of 3. The right hand then moves to deposit its 3 stitches followed by the left. Left-handed knitters will reverse the process (Fig. 54).

On the Passap, when you have taken the first lot of stitches off the needles, tilt the tool sideways so that it lies behind the second one as it removes its 3 stitches for the transfer. Push the tools firmly in a straight line aligned with the needle shank. Do not hesitate. If you have difficulty because of nervousness in flicking open the latches, put the lint brush between your teeth and use the bristles as latch openers. You now have a third hand, which is very useful indeed in the production of cables.

In the 1860s (so the story goes) Isaac Lamb, the American inventor of a nineteenth century knitting machine, prayed: 'Dear Lord, impart to it the dexterity of the hand'. He could have prayed more meaningfully: 'Impart to the machine knitter dexterity and co-ordination of hand and machine'.

5 Tuck—a stitch for a king

A hand knitter is as likely to tackle a crunchy tuck stitch as a machine knitter is likely to hand-tool a garter stitch. Brioche or fisherman's rib stitches remain popular with experienced hand knitters, but there must be very few who would wish to labour under the repetitive chore of dropping and unravelling stitches 4 to 6 rows down, and then picking up and knitting off the stitch below and its unravelled strands. One can safely say that tuck stitch remains the almost exclusive preserve of the machine knitter and that the origins to search for are to be found in industrial and mechanised knitting.

Tuck stitch has an unsolved mystery about its beginnings, which is as intriguing as that surrounding Fair Isle or Aran. For almost two hundred years plain stocking stitch was knitted on the hand frame, and then (we think) in late 1730s came the invention of the tucking bar, which proved to be a most versatile acquisition. Framework knitters could then knit a vertical self-coloured pattern, which had the appearance of mock rib, and so increased the attractiveness of their stocking tops. One of the first tuck patterns must have been Knitmaster Card 7, J & B and Toyota Card 2 and Passap AX, alternating pushers and left arrow key down on the front lock. Try changing colours every two rows. Please note that the card is not in the J & B 881 pack.

What the tucking bar did was precisely what the tucking cam does on the modern machine. It allowed the tucking needle to advance far enough forward to grasp a loop of yarn, but not to withdraw to the point where a stitch could be formed. Eventually, after several tuck loops were laid in the needlehead, the stitch was knitted and the bubbly, crunchy texture of tuck emerged.

Gravenor Henson, writing in his *History of the Framework Knitters* (1831), has an interesting and quaint definition: 'A tuck stitch is where the stitch is unlooped in a single stitch; it is a defect only to the eye, in the beauty of the fabric the work is equally sound. Learners and unskilful persons are apt to make tuck stitches.'

Henson goes on to tell us that tuck was invented in the late 1730s and that the inventor was either an Irishman or Louis XIV of France, who was an accomplished framework knitter and who did not suffer from any aesthetic inhibitions where the use of machinery was concerned. The story goes that the King even worked his machine in the Palace of Versailles. Henson leaves us in no doubt that his choice is 'Lewis the Fourteenth'. The problem is that *le roi soleil* died in 1715. Modern British hand frame scholars also favour Louis XIV as the inventor and think that the tucking bar was in use before the 1730s, though how such a valuable commercial asset remained a secret for 20 years or so is very puzzling. The mystery remains unsolved, but one thing is sure: the inventor was not an Englishman.

Description of tuck stitch

Tuck stitch is enormously versatile and unlimited pattern variations are possible. Manual tuck patterns can be done on most machines by pushing selected needles to hold for several rows, before pushing the needles back to U W P to knit off the loops. Pull-up tuck stitch has a slightly more pronounced look than the usual loop-in-the-latch-head method. The most pronounced tuck stitch of all is that produced by the stripper system on the Passap. The loops are held in the needle heads, but the strippers do not flatten the stitch. They allow the tuck loops to bubble out and create an unrivalled textured pattern (Fig. 55).

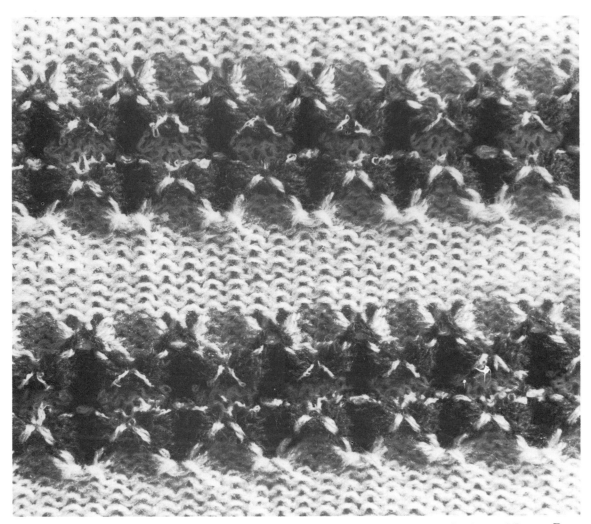

Figure 55. Basic single bed honeycomb tuck

While there may be some doubt about tuck being the exclusive preserve of the machine knitter, there is no doubt at all about plated knitting. This is exclusively a machine method and was invented in the late 1760s by Robert Ash of Nottingham. Plating (sometimes misspelt plaiting in Japanese manuals) is the even and regular layering of a contrast yarn over the main yarn in the knitting. The result is a stitch which gives an illusion of even greater depth and beauty.

Tuck stitches can be simple and based on a small regular repeat, which thickens the fabric considerably. Alternatively, they can form large, bold geometrics which project from the knitted base like filigree tracery. It is this type of pattern combined with plating which has been chosen for the garment in this section. Every-other-needle tuck is a possibility with heavy yarns. The simplest pattern to use

as a starter is Knitmaster Card 2 and Passap Deco Card 18 (Fig. 56). Cast on and knit tuck over every alternate needle. In this category are the so-called Aran Tucks, which simulate the more famous hand-knitting stitches (Fig. 57). Tuck lace (Fig. 58) is another fascinating area, where the tucking needle is isolated by adjacent needles pushed back to NWP position. The strands bridging the space create a beautiful, lace-like structure. Some of the loveliest effects in tuck stitch are achieved not only by the contrast of colour, but by the contrast of thick and thin; yarn with thread.

It is easy to rhapsodise over tuck stitch, as indeed one can over many stitches of which the machine is capable. The question is: What do you do with tuck stitch? It is often difficult to decide. Some knitters fight shy of it, knowing that an all-over tuck stitch will produce a row and stitch tension as far removed from stocking stitch as any stitch can be, for there are

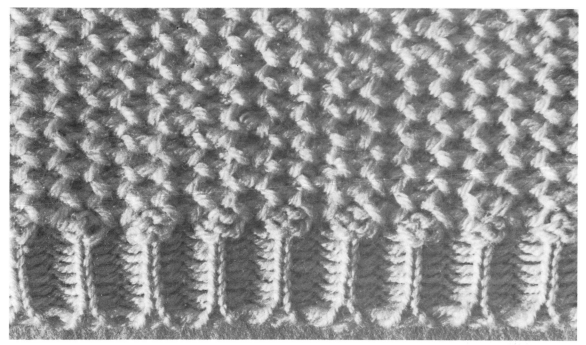

Figure 56. Every-other-needle tuck (Knitmaster card 2, Passap Deco card 18)

Figure 57. Every-other-needle Aran-type tuck. (Knitmaster set 1011, card M198)

always fewer stitches and more rows to 10 cm. Other knitters are perplexed by tuck-stock stitches (tuck alternating with stocking stitch rows). These stitches produce even more rows per 10 cm than a straightforward tuck, but have the advantage of looking as good – if not better – on the knit side than the purl side of the fabric, whereas most tucks produce a purl side/right side fabric (Fig. 59). The answer, of course, is to employ the charting device, for knitters can never find written patterns in the tuck stitch of their choice.

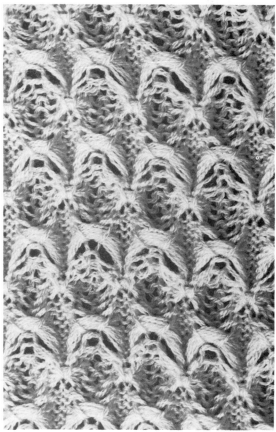

Figure 58. Tuck lace (Passap Deco card 17)

47

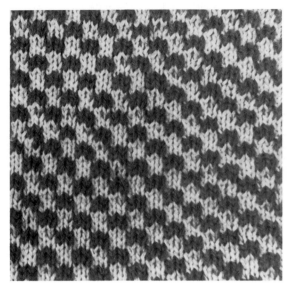

Figure 59. Two-colour 'pop-corn' tuck stitch
(Knitmaster card 2, Passap Deco card 18)

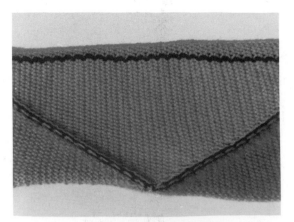

Figure 60. Intarsia tuck using holding position

Figure 61. Double bed tuck (pusher pattern – Passap
Duo)

It is also true that tuck stitch fabric has curly edges
that are difficult to sew in a straight seam. The fronts
on a tuck stitch jacket have an irritating habit of
flipping over, and one needs to know the best type of
band to use. Moreover, one can appreciate why many
craft knitters choose to use only small areas of tuck to
contrast with single bed Fair Isle, lace, weaving or
simply stocking stitch. Why then bother to press the
case for allover tuck garments? No one should
attempt to put a fence around any craft; the sky is the
limit. How many knitters have experimented with
multi-coloured intarsia tuck? (Fig. 60). There must
be very few. Additionally, not many knitters have
ventured into the area of double bed tucks (Figs 61
and 62). The moral is, of course, that until a
discipline is learnt and practised, interesting and
inventive variations do not and cannot emerge. In
short, it is far easier to close the lid on a trunk full of
tuck stitch samples than it is to know what use to put
them to at the end of a knitting day.

The pattern-shape and techniques of knitting

The garment design is formal and classic, for the
simple reason that the plated tuck pattern should be
shown to the fullest possible advantage. The original
colours were wheaten gold over deep salmon pink. It
is hoped that the pattern will help knitters tackle
features they could well avoid on garments of their
own choice – namely, pockets in a patterned fabric,
sideways knitted and finished buttonholes and bands
on a tuck jacket (Fig. 63). If you do not have plating

facilities on your machine, there is no reason why you
cannot just do a plain self-coloured tuck. For plating,
fine counts are necessary, and the plating yarn which
is threaded into the plating feeder is the one which
emerges on top of the main yarn. Though it is taken
first by the needle, it performs a somersault in the
stitch-making process and ends up facing the knitter.
Practise with contrast yarns before making your
choice, trying first one in the plating feeder and then
the other. Plating can produce weird as well as
wonderful colour combinations in fabric.

Three strands of $\frac{2}{30}$ industrial yarn make an approximate fine 4-ply in weight. Put one strand in the

48

Cap-sleeved lace blouse (Chapter 7)

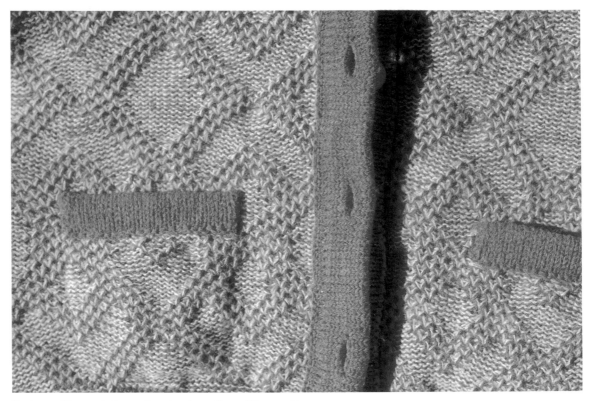

Pocket and buttonhole on plated tuck cardigan (Chapter 5)

Jones & Brother three-colour-in-a-row Jacquard (Chapter 9)

Figure 62. Double bed tuck – fantasy jacquard (Passap Deco card 3)

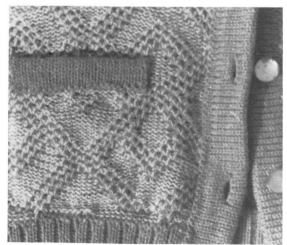

Figure 63. Pocket and buttonhole band

plating feeder and two in the main. Incidentally, plating also helps eliminate the dropped loops which can occur on the tuck setting when using stranded yarns. If two ends of yarn have a strong twist in them and misbehave on stocking stitch by knitting on a slight bias, then separate them and put one in the plating feeder and one in the main; $\frac{2}{16}$ English crossbred wool is best dealt with in this way, if there is an over twist in the yarn.

The machine used is the Brother 910 Electroknit. The pattern is given for S K 500 owners who wish to copy it (Fig. 64) identically. Passap and punchcard machine owners should choose a suitable alternative. Passap owners who have a four-colour changer can get a plating effect by feeding two yarns through number 1 tension mast and one yarn through number 4 tension mast. All three yarns go into the same eyelet 'bullet'. Please note the reversal principle which is commonly associated with tuck and slip patterns. On a punch card, the blank area represents the needle to be tucked (the opposite on the Toyota 787) and the hole represents the needle knitting plain. This necessitates a lot of punching. On the electronic machines a button reverses the procedure and ensures that the same marking method applies for all pattern stitches. The Passap arrow key reverses the

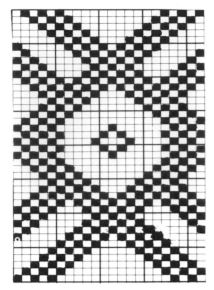

Figure 64. Pattern 2–10, Brother 910

Figure 65. Child's plated tuck jacket

pushers. Therefore pattern delineation on the Deco card follows the principle of the Japanese electronic machines.

Child's Plated Tuck Jacket

Size
To fit 71 cm (28″) chest. Actual measurement 81 cm (32″).

Materials
175 g (7 oz) main colour (2 ends), 75 g (3 oz) second colour (plating yarn) $\frac{2}{30}$ courtelle – wool. 7 buttons.

Tension
25 sts – 58 rows per 10 cm. 15.8 cm per 40 sts. 10.3 cm per 60 rows. T5.2 (Passap Duo St.s $5\frac{3}{4}$).

Machine used
Brother Electroknit 910. Pattern no. 2 (2–10). Buttons 4 and 6 in up position (elongation). Use KC1. SK500 use button 3. Other machines – choose an appropriate pattern.

Back

Single bed machines
Using WY and 2 × 1 mock rib cast on 100 sts. Knit 6rs in WY. Change to MY (3 ends of $\frac{2}{30}$) and T.3. Knit 24 rs. 1 fold row on T.7. Change to T.3 knit 24 rs. Complete welt.

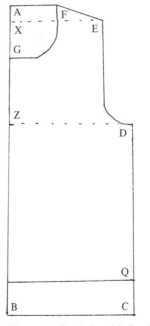
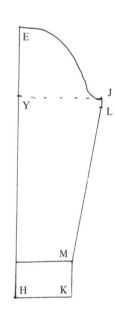

Figure 66. Block for child's plated tuck jacket.

Back/front	ZD	=	$\frac{1}{4}$ chest + ease = 18 cm (7 in)
	AB	=	44 cm (17$\frac{1}{2}$ in)
	XZ	=	15 cm (6 in)
	AF	=	13 cm (5$\frac{1}{4}$ in)
	XE	=	28 cm (11 in)
	AG	=	7.5 cm (3 in)
	AX	=	1.25 cm ($\frac{1}{2}$ in)
Sleeve	EH	=	39.5 cm (15$\frac{1}{2}$ in)
	EY	=	10 cm (4 in)
	YJ	=	25 cm (10 in)
	JL	=	1 cm ($\frac{1}{2}$ in)
	M	=	16.5 cm (6$\frac{1}{2}$ in)
	KM	=	5 cm (2 in)

Figure 67. Pocket slit knitted over with waste yarn

Double bed machines and ribber

Using $3 \times \frac{2}{30}$ MY and 1×1 rib $T\frac{2}{3}$. Knit 24 rows.

All machines

Thread 1 end of plating yarn through plating feed and place 2 ends of MY in main feed. T.5.2. Arrange for pattern. Set to tuck. Knit to row 134. Carr at right RC 000.

Armholes

CO 4 at beg of next 2 rows. CO 2 at beg of next 2 rows. CO 1 at beg of next 6 rows. * Knit 2 rows. CO 1 at beg of next 2 rows. Repeat 4 rows from * 3 times in all. (76 sts) RC 22. Knit straight to shoulders RC 108.

Shoulders

Dec over 10 rows (5 rows at each side) CO 5 sts at beg of next 2 rows, ** CO 4 sts at beg of next 2 rows. Repeat from * 4 times altogether. 34 sts remain. Scrap off on WY. Release from machine.

Right front

Cast on 50 sts at right of 0 on needle bed. Welt and pattern arrangement as for back. RC 000 Knit plated tuck to RC 41. Carr at left.

Pocket

Counting from the 13th to 36th needle right of 0 and using a length of WY and the buttonhole method, knit off manually the selected 23 sts. Knit to R 134 (133 for left front). Carr at right. RC 000 (Fig. 67).

Armhole

CO 4 sts at beg of next row. Knit 1 row. Co 2 sts at beg of next row. Knit 1 row. CO 1 stitch at beg of next and every alt row 3 times altogether. *Knit 3 rows. CO 1 stitch at beg of next row. Rep. 4 rows 3 times in all. RC 21. Carr at left (38 sts) Knit straight to Row 66. Carr at right.

Front neck

Take off onto a double eyed bodkin threaded with WY 9 sts at extreme left. Knit to left. CO 3 sts at beg of next row. Knit 1 row. CO 2 sts at beg of next row. Knit 1 row. CO 1 stitch at beg of next and every alt row, 3 times in all (21 sts remain). Knit straight to row 108.

Shoulder

As for back, but decrease on every alt row at right. CO (1 row in 2 rows) 5, 4 × 4 sts (21 sts).

Left front

As right, but follow instructions for left and read left for right.

Sleeve

Cast on 40 sts. Welt as for back but use T.4. Change to T.5.2 and pattern RC 000. Inc 1 stitch at each end of next and following 9th row 16 times altogether (72 sts). RC 136. Knit straight to row 150. Adjust. RC 000.

Armhole and sleeve cap

CO 4 sts at beg of next 2 rows. CO 2 sts at beg of next 2 rows. CO 1 stitch at beg of next 10 rows. * Knit 2 rows. Dec 1 stitch at beg of next 2 rows. Repeat 4 rows from * 10 times in all (RC 54). Dec 1 stitch at beg of next 6 rows. CO 3 sts at beg of next 4 rows. CO remaining 12 stitches.

Pocket

Hemmed top: right side of fabric facing pick up 23 stitches below WY row. Using $3 \times \frac{2}{30}$ MY, T.4.2. Knit 8 rows stocking stitch. T.7 fold row. T4.2 knit 8 rows. Change to WY knit 8 rows. Release. Do other pocket the same. Passap – use back bed.

Lining

On wrong side of the fabric, fold over top part of piece above pocket opening, neck to face the machine. Pick up 23 sts above WY. T.5.2. Knit 28 rows. Cast off loosely. Remove WY. Do other side the same.

Turn pocket top onto right side and back stitch into first row of MY sts above WY. Remove WY. Stitch sides of hemmed top. Catch lining down on the inside, taking care to follow vertical line of stitches. Do not let stitching show on the right side.

Neck

Stitch up shoulder seams. With right side of fabric facing pick up 92 stitches. Remove WY. Using $3 \times \frac{2}{30}$ MY, knit 2 rows at T.6. Arrange for rib or single bed welt.

Single bed welt

Knit 4 rows at T.3.2., 4 rows at T.3.1., 4 rows at T.3. Fold row at T.6. Reverse.

Rib

4 rows at $T.\frac{3}{4}$. 4 rows at $T.\frac{2.2}{3.2}$, 4 rows at $T.\frac{2.1}{3.1}$. Fold row $T\frac{5}{6}$. Reverse.

All machines

Arrange for stocking stitch at T.6. Pick up stitches from 2nd row of st st below rib/welt and place on needles to close the rib/welt. Knit 2 rows. Scrap off in WY (6 rows). Back stitch band in place as for pocket top. Remove waste yarn.

Button band (stocking stitch)

Pick up 120 sts evenly along band (8 for neck, 96 along main piece, 16 for welt). RC 000. T.4.2. knit 11 rows stocking stitch, fold row on T.6.2. T.4.2. Knit 11 rows. Pick up sts from first row of band. T.5.2. knit 2 rows to close band. Scrap off in WY (6 rows). Stitch down as for pocket top. Remove W.Y.

Buttonhole band (stocking stitch)

Row calculation and knitting as for button band. On row 6 make 7 buttonholes over groups of 4 needles with space of 14 ns between. Use WY to knit off manually the groups of 4 sts. Buttonhole stitches are in brackets: 4,(4), 14,(4), 14,(4). 14,(4), 14,(4), 14,(4), 14,(4), 4 = 120 stitches. Knit 5 rows. Fold row on T7.1. Knit 5 rows. Counting from the right, push ns 5,6,7,8, forward slightly. The diagram (Fig. 68) represents the stitches in WY, 11 rows below. The dotted line is WY. The unbroken line represents the loops of MY stitches. On the top line, there are 1 half loop, 3 loops, 1 half loop, 1 × and 5 × being the half loops.

Figure 68. Diagram showing how to make a buttonhole

* Lift up 1 × and place on needle 5. 11 rows above and to the left. Slip st over 1 ×. With one-eyed transfer tool, transfer st from needle 6 onto needle 5. Place in front of 1 ×. Holding firmly with finger and thumb to separate, slip 1 × over st from needle 6. Transfer back to needle 6. Pick up 2 ×. Place in front of st on needle 7 and repeat process until 4 ns are empty. Pick up 5 × and place on needle 9 (2 loops on 9). Lift loops 1, 2, 3, 4 onto empty needles. **

Repeat buttonhole procedure along row * to ** 7 times in all. Complete as for button band.

To complete

Remove all WY. Stitch sleeve into place by hand to prevent warpage. Using sewing machine and a medium zigzag stitch, close sleeve seams and side seams. Neaten welts. Sew on buttons. Give the garment a light cool press, if necessary.

Notes

1. This tuck pattern is a 2-row pattern and the elongation device must be used in the original Electroknit pattern. Passap Duomatic owners – try Deco card 19, Selector dial on 2, single bed AX pattern. Punch card owners have plenty of choice. The problem is how to deal with mistakes when the elongation device is in operation. On the punchcard machines and the Passap Duomatic machine, pull back to the right hand side. On the Electroknit, the mechanism can operate from right or left, not just from the right. The important point is pull back to the side where the card moves on for the next row and then take the memory. Brother, Singer and Toyota knitters must pre-select before they can pattern knit.

2. The most common yarn available in the $\frac{2}{30}$s count is all-acrylic. If you search around coned yarn centres, you may find wool-acrylic mixes, pure $\frac{2}{24}$ wool and $\frac{2}{24}$ bright silky acrylics. Fine silky yarns used on the plated tuck setting achieve a rich, brocaded appearance reminiscent of the superb Spanish and Italian knitting of the sixteenth and seventeenth centuries (Fig. 69). Always do a tension swatch before knitting and use a basic fitted sleeve shape on the charting device.

3. Two methods of tension measuring are given in these patterns. The majority of knitting authorities use the stitches and rows per 10 cm formula. Brother, Singer (Juki) and Toyota, however, instruct their charting device knitters to measure in cm and mm between the 40 sts and 60 rows of their swatch. Here are the equations for conversion. X is the unknown quantity.

Stitch

(a) 15.8 cm = 40 sts
     10 cm = X
(b) 15.8 X = 400
(c)   X = $\frac{400}{15.8}$
(d)   X = 25 sts

The method operates in reverse:
(a) 25 sts = 10 cm
     40 sts = X
(b) 25 X = 400
(c)   X = $\frac{400}{25}$
(d)   X = 15.8 cm

Row

(a) 10.3 cm = 60 rows
     10 cm = X
(b) 10.3 X = 600
(c)   X = $\frac{600}{10.3}$
(d)   X = 58 rows.

(a) 58 rows = 10 cm
     60 rows = X
(b) 58 X = 600
(c)   X = $\frac{600}{58}$
(d)   = 10.3 cm

The quickest way is to place a Knitmaster green ruler alongside a metric ruler and read off the stitches and rows per 10 cm against the given measurement. Passap knitters can find the 10 cm readings in the charts given in the instruction manual or in the Passap ABC. The 10 cm readings are also presented as a chart in the last chapter of this book (Fig. 196).

4. How do you calculate the stitches to be picked up for the front bands? There are various methods you can try. The simplest is to stretch the piece out in front of the machine and pick up evenly all the way along, though it is not easy to achieve a balanced pick-up on patterned fabrics. With stocking stitch garments it is not difficult to measure the front and convert it to stitches for the band. This works well even though the band is on a tighter tension than the main fabric (usually one whole number lower). The other method is to work through the row and stitch ratio, so for 32 sts 48 rows per 10 cm you pick up

2 out of 3 edge loops and stitch knobs.

Any pattern fabric with a row and stitch tension as different as can be from stocking stitch presents a problem. For this pattern a swatch was worked out in the band fabric. At T.4.2, it produced 28 sts and 43 rows per 10 cm. The measurement along the front of 34.5 cm, converted to stitches, produced 120 sts, of which 96 came from the main pattern. The ratio of 25 sts to 58 rows decreed that 1 stitch should be picked up for 2.3 rows. In the main fabric, from above the welt to the neck, there are 200 rows. When this sum was worked out the answer was 96 sts, the same as the other.

5. The practice of picking up a row below to seal the bands in the neck and the fronts has the effect of firming the fabric and minimising the flip over of the fronts. There are several ways to knit a pocket; this is one of the easiest. Equally, there are various versions of the finished buttonhole and this one is the most

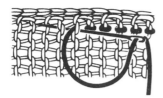

Figure 70. Backstitch

popular. It is fortunate that the buttonhole calculations work out equally (14 sts between each buttonhole). If there are odd stitches, distribute them, so that the buttonholes are nearest together where there is most strain from the wearer.

6. Please note that the welt tension for the sleeves is one whole number looser than on the back and the fronts. This is due to the fact that there are fewer stitches per 10 cm on tuck than on stocking stitch. The number of stitches is determined by the pattern, and in this case there may not be enough to provide a comfortable fit on the wrist, so the stitch tension must be looser.

A good double bed rib to use in conjunction with tuck is the 2 × 1 industrial rib, because there is one-third more stitches than on a 1 × 1 rib. The extra number provide for a rib welt that is the ideal accompaniment to tuck. The card can be put in the machine during the welt. Knitmaster owners can forget it until the time comes to pattern-knit. When the welt is complete, Brother, Singer (Juki) and Toyota knitters must preselect for the pattern. The best way is to free-slip to the left and then slip pattern to the right to collect the yarn. For slip, the Brother machine has the part buttons and the Toyota the 'empty' setting. The selected needles come to D position and pattern-knitting can begin.

7. *Single bed welts and the new knitter.* Instruction books outline casting on methods, but they do not always state clearly how these methods can be applied in the knitting of welts. The 2 × 1 welt is the one knitters use most. The 1 × 1 in 3- and 4-ply yarn produces a flabby result and this setting is best kept for double knitting yarn. New knitters often ask for advice on how to knit a welt. Waste yarn and the nylon ravel cord feature in the two most popular methods.

(a) All single bed machines. Cast on in MT with WY. Knit 1 row. Lay the nylon cord over the inside of the sinker pins just below the needle heads. Hold both ends of the cord very firmly and knit across with the carriage six times (Knitmaster – side levers

Figure 69. Left Seventeenth-century Venetian tunic in green and gold silk. (Victoria and Albert Museum)

Figure 71. Holding the nylon cord

forward). If you do not hold the ends firmly enough, the nylon cord will not stay in place (Fig. 71). Remove the nylon cord at the end of 6 rows. Brother and Toyota machines – hang the comb according to the instruction book. There is no need to use the nylon cord (Fig. 72).

(b) *All single bed machines with built-in weaving brushes.* Use WY as for the cast on in Method 1. Push out to HP 1 needle in every pair of working position needles. The o represents a needle in non-working position.

$$| \quad | \quad O \quad | \quad | \quad O \quad | \quad | \quad O \quad | \quad | \quad O \quad | \quad |$$

Insert the yarn into the carriage feed. Set the cams to knit the needles back. Lay the end of the yarn across the needles in working position as shown in the instruction book. Put the weaving brushes down. Knit across. Lift up the weaving brushes to non-working position. Knit six rows in waste yarn. Carriage at right. Knitmaster side levers should be forward. Brother machines – the casting-on comb can also be hung for this method to give additional pull down (Fig. 74).

The next stage. This applies to both methods. Hang the claw weights at the edges. Take the waste yarn out of the feed. Insert the nylon cord, fastening one end to the clamp and holding the other end above the feed. Knit to left. Remove end of nylon cord and leave. Change to main yarn and welt tension, usually main tension − 3. RC 000. Knitmaster – side levers back. Knit depth of welt, say 24 rows. Knit 1 row on main tension + 1 for fold. Change to welt tension, main tension + 3. Knit 24 rows. RC 49, carriage at right. Push all in-between needles to working position for full complement. Lift up welt and pick up loops above nylon cord, placing loops on 2 out of 3

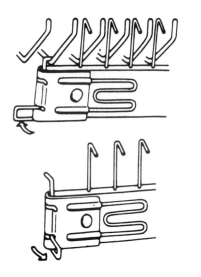

Figure 72. Suspending the Brother casting-on comb

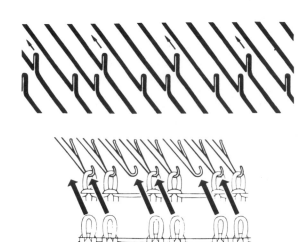

Figure 73. Completing a 2 × 1 welt

Figure 74. Weaving cast on

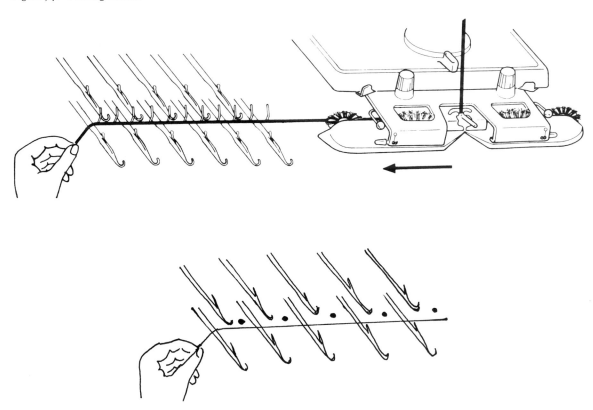

56

needles along the row, always seeing that the empty needle receives a loop to prevent a hole (Fig. 73).

When the bottom edge loops are all picked up, push the needles to holding position. Set the cams to knit them back. Stitch dial to main tension. RC 000 and begin to knit the main part.

After 30–40 rows remove the nylon cord and waste knitting by pulling the nylon cord along and out. The waste yarn should fall away leaving a perfectly executed welt.

The position of the Knitmaster side levers (punchcard models)

When they are forward, the needles do not advance to take the yarn until they are under the carriage. Have the levers forward until the fabric is long enough for the brushes and fabric pressers to take a grip. Then put the side levers back to the normal knitting and patterning position.

6 The raglan and the perfect finish

Lord Raglan, commander in chief of the British troops in the Crimean War (1853–6), gave his name to one of the most casual and comfortable of sleeve styles in knitwear. Originally, a raglan referred to one-piece sleeve and shoulders in overcoats. The raglan seam affords an easy loose fit ideally suited for a coat which has to go over other garments. Whether this practical wartime style had any large scale impact on Victorian male dress remains a matter for conjecture, but it is a fact that between 1850 and 1860 male over-dress lost the cape or mantle and took on its modern, streamlined look, which is more than can be said of the female garb of the period. A block pattern for an overcoat (dated 1858) in Carl Köhler's *History of Costume* (Dover) shows quite clearly that though the front part of the sleeve is fitted, the back has a raglan shaping, a style we can still see on some commercial knitwear of today.

Like other garment features now very much a part of the modern knitting scene, the raglan was submerged beneath other more popular fashion styles until the 1930s, when raglan seams (back, front and sleeves) began to appear in the new knitwear fashion 'glossies'. Raglans were for easy movement, and were suited to the vigorous lifestyle of the twentieth century (Fig. 75).

Though Mary Thomas, in her *Knitting Book*, never mentions the raglan block, the decade of the 1930s was the period when knitting designers explored silhouettes as well as pattern stitches. It had never been done before. During the 1940s, however, the Second World War temporarily put an end to adventurous investigation of shape. The squared look and the puffed sleeve ensured that the raglan was again out of favour, though just occasionally one comes across instructions and a diagram in publi-

cations of the time illustrating how one could design and knit a raglan.

The 1950s heralded more relaxed styles. To counteract the all-pervasive 'classic' influence of Chanel other designers introduced, as a fashion knit, the dolman or batwing sweater. In the issues of Knitmaster's *Modern Knitting* in the late 1950s the full sleeved dolman is sometimes called 'the jumper with Magyar sleeves'. Designers are often influenced by current and past popular interests and the associated visual stimuli. With the discovery of Tutankhamun's tomb in the early 1920s it was noted that the ancient Egyptians wore slim-skirted gauzy tunics with dolman-type sleeves decorated with fabulous jewelled collars, which, 30 years later, were often interpreted by knitting designers as chevron-shaped Fair Isle patterns high on the shoulders near the throat (Fig. 76). If the dolmans were knitted

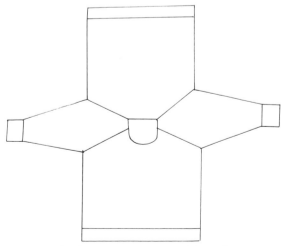

Figure 75. Raglan garment outline (all-in-one)

Figure 76. 1950s–60s – Raglan-dolman with patterned yoke

Figure 77. 1960s–70s – Sideways knitted dolman with vertical bands of patterning

sideways, as they often were on the machine, then the Fair Isle or coloured tuck would appear as flattering vertical stripes in the area where the sleeve merged into the main back and front of the garment (Fig. 77).

Modern Knitting and the *Passap Pattern Book* concentrated at first on fitted sleeves, the dolman and the traditional dropped shoulder line, but these were gradually accompanied by the raglan shape. By the mid-fifties, the raglan had arrived and was beginning to be accepted as the easiest-to-knit and easiest-to-wear of all casuals. Machine knitters explored a wide variety of raglan patterns and edges using their transfer tools to make a number of fully-fashioned shapings. The simplest way to make a raglan decrease is to decrease one stitch at the very edge of the garment piece. With the three-eyed transfer tool, and indeed, a combination of transfer tools, knitters could ring the changes. Sometimes the stitches were decreased two or more at a time. Occasionally, a lacy effect was employed by decreasing two stitches and leaving one needle empty, so that in fact only one decrease was made. A sharp, smooth raglan edge was achieved by moving the stitches outwards towards the edge and then back again towards the centre of the garment (Fig. 78).

The late 1950s and early 1960s saw the emergence of a raglan style which was one of the most interesting to knit on a simple machine with holding cam levers but no automatic patterning system (Fig. 79). This garment was the all-in-one, integral or hung – as it is called by machine knitters in the U.S.A. – raglan. The style remained popular until the early 1970s and then disappeared from magazines (apart from the *Passap Baby Book*) until interest in this method of knitting revived more recently, especially among industrial designers. The arrival of automated patterning, and new coned yarns which do not get the old tensions quite so easily, contributed to the decline of the all-in-one raglan, but it was the charting device more than anything which was responsible for the near disappearance of the all-in-one raglan in the early 1970s. The dominance first of the fitted sleeve pattern and then of the dropped shoulder line meant that raglans, whether they were constructed all-in-one or of several pieces, took a back seat in the fashion scene once more, but they never lost their popularity as school and casual wear. Moreover, it became apparent that raglan diagonals presented a problem to charting device owners on certain row and stitch tensions. The only way to ensure even and regular

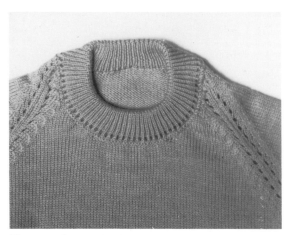

Figure 78. Lacy raglan effect

decreases, it was discovered, was to work them out mathematically, because the charting device could not always be relied on to give automatic readings of regularity. This problem we have now grappled with and at least can offer a partial solution. The charting device rulers and readings are used by the knitter to work out the decreases for the number of stitches and rows given. The pattern of decreases may change, but at least it can be organised that the change takes place at the same point on all the garment pieces.

In the early to mid 1970s this problem turned many experienced knitters away from the charting device. They preferred to stay with the written patterns they knew so well or to work out any anomalies with the aid of mental arithmetic, a pencil and paper and, latterly, a calculator. Now, not only has the use of the charting device become a habit, but we are also in a period of fashion when nearly anything goes, and are free once more to investigate some of the shapes which have evolved from the versatile raglan.

It must be said, however, that the raglan is not a favourite shape with many of today's fashion designers; the reason is very clear. The raglan diagonals can act like a guillotine across patterns and a decapitated pattern across the front of a garment can be very disconcerting. There are, however, some patterns with very strong vertical and horizontal interest

Figure 79. The Passap M201, 1953. (Passap, Switzerland)

which thrive on being diverted down or across the sleeve. Today, it is not what the raglan is, but what it has become, that is of significance.

Ironically, it is the mastery of the charting device which leaves free to consider the evolution of the raglan shape. The raglan-dolman, circular yoke top and the raglan saddle are three of the shapes developed from the basic block for use on dresses and coats as well as on sweaters and jackets. These are some of the principles which could form the groundwork for the study of fully-fashioned knit. Such a discipline could well have far reaching results in the knitwear industry and in the colleges which train our designers. One aspect is worthy of comment: the revival of interest in the all-in-one or integral raglan is not confined by any means to domestic knitters. In the last few years a British invention called the presser foot has made a revolutionary impact on industrial knitting. The presser foot allows the garment to be shaped as it is knitted, so that as many making-up seams as possible are eliminated on a garment that must be speedily accomplished to remain competitive in price. Moreover, all-in-one or integral garments can be knitted automatically on the latest industrial machines. The hand tooling of the home knitter has, through automation, become a very rapid process indeed. It is interesting that many of the finishing techniques despised by the craft knitter for whom design, colour and texture are everything, should now be the object of the keenest scrutiny by the industrial designer, who wants his product to resemble the hand-made, hand-finished article as nearly as possible. While some cut and sew techniques are employed by those operating in the domestic scene, many craft knitters realise that they can only hope for up-market sales if they ensure that their products are one-offs and cannot be copied so easily by modern industrial technology. If adorning knitwear by decorative touches is one method, then perfectionist methods of finishing constitute another. This does not rule out the use of the sewing machine, linker or overlocker, but it is rare to find exclusive hand-crafted knitwear executed completely by cut-and-sew methods.

Raglan Finishes

There is something about the unadorned raglan shape which invites the knitter to employ the neatest possible finish in the making up. Raglans can be very boring, especially to those who have to knit several before the opening of a new school year. It is worthwhile looking through the old manuals in search of interesting and unusual details; it is surprising how many original collars, cuffs, bands and pockets there were on classic garments, for example.

The figure-of-eight graft

In the Knitmaster 3500 instruction book, dated mid-1950s, there is described a technique known as the figure-of-eight graft. The 3500 instruction book was the only manual used by students at the first ever adult education class in machine knitting, held in Liverpool during 1957. The graft was never published again until the instructions were printed in my first *Resource Book for Machine Knitters*. The technique survived as an oral tradition, because the practice of using the figure-of-eight graft is still very common in the north-west of England, especially in the making up of classic, fully fashioned four-piece raglans. The finishes taught at that Liverpool class were taken to New Zealand in 1962 by Mrs Alice Day of Wellington. The international reputation New Zealand has for its exceptionally high standard in machine knitting, a standard which is upheld by its unique national machine knitters' society, is due in no small way to that first class in Liverpool.

It is interesting, however, that the figure-of-eight graft does not appear amongst the fully-fashioned techniques practised by the Swiss who plan the *Passap International Model Books*, nor by the Japanese, who are rapidly establishing *Nihon Vogue*, *Brother* and *Silver Seiko Fashion Knit* publications as the most influential of their kind in the world. The Knitmaster 3500 manual, like its accompanying machine, was a British production. Among its ancestors were the Victorian domestic machine and the old hand frame manuals.

Techniques of the figure-of-eight graft

This technique may seem rather exacting at first; many knitters will not take kindly to having to sit at the machine to complete a garment. It is indeed a matter of choice. Those who have mastered the figure-of-eight are grateful for a technique which gives them beautifully made-up knitwear. Moreover, those who have been taught to hand tool and work at the machine more than is considered necessary are more likely to forge a harmonious relationship with the machine than knitters for whom it is just the speedy means to an end. This applies whether the knitters continue to use the techniques regularly or just for the special occasion. The grounding has been given and it remains for ever an invaluable asset. It is a pity we cannot know the opinion of the Rev. William Lee on this overturning of the traditional view of the machine. The seventeenth century coat of arms of the London Framework Knitters may be

Figure 80. The coat of arms of the London Framework Knitters Guild, 1663

interesting for the clues it gives on early sock knitting, but it is even more interesting on another count. There William Lee stands, flanking his frame on one side. His wife, with her discarded hand knitting in her hand, stands on the other. Together, they celebrate one concept – speed (Fig. 80).

The beautiful flat crochet-like finish of the figure-of-eight graft forms a more natural, elastic link between pieces in a fibre art project than any finish given by the sewing machine, linker or overlocker. At the other end of the spectrum, the graft provides the flattest seam there is for socks, but then knitting is like that; the sublime and the ridiculous, the exalted and the mundane can co-exist very happily in the experience of one knitter. Variations of the figure-of-eight graft produce decorative edges which people find hard to distinguish from real crochet (Fig. 81). I use the graft when I want a special effect in a small area. The collar pieces in the pattern were put back

Figure 81. Crochet edge made by the figure-of-eight graft

onto the machine, the waste yarn removed and the two lots of stitches joined with the figure-of-eight (Fig. 82). They could have been crocheted together for a similar effect. The photographs which illustrate the graft show it being used to link together the side seams of a skirt, the two pieces of which were knitted sideways and the stitches cast off after a slack row. The grafted side seams were perfect inside and out and beautifully flat. The graft can be executed at either the right- or left-hand side of the machine.

Instructions for the figure-of-eight graft

1. Hook the edge loops of one knitted piece (right side facing) onto the needles of the machine. With the wrong side facing, hitch up the edge loops (or stitches) of the second knitted piece. Two loops are on each needle (Fig. 83).

2. Place a ball or cone of the main yarn on the floor beside you. As a rough guess, six times the equivalent length of the knitting to be grafted will be required. Start at the side you find best. Make a slip knot. Hitch

Figure 82. Fringed collar

Figure 83. Figure-of-eight: stage 1

Figure 84. Figure-of-eight: stage 2

Figure 85. Figure-of-eight: stage 3

Figure 86. Figure-of-eight: stage 4

it onto the open hook of the second needle. Push the two stitches or loops already on the needle behind the latch. Knit them off by laying the end of yarn in the needle head. There is one loop left. This is only a starter to anchor the yarn safely (Fig. 84).

3. The needles are all back to normal. Take the long end of the yarn and lay it over the open latch of the first needle. Push the two stitches or loops behind the latch of the first needle. Draw the needle back to close the latch and knit off the stitches. When you do the crocheted edge, using the figure-of-eight method, repeat this operation three or four times (Fig. 85).

4. Now, with a one-eyed latch tool, approach the loop on the first needle from behind, coming towards yourself with the eye of the tool, 'as if you are going to stab yourself', in the words of one teacher. Slip the eyed-shank of the tool through the loop and push it and the needle towards you (needle comes to UWP). Hold the fabric beneath with fingers and thumb firmly, with a little downward pressure (Fig. 86).

Figure 87. Figure-of-eight: stage 5

5. Ease the yarn a little as you move, drawing it up into a bigger loop. Now bring your hand over and down to twist the loop into a figure-of-eight. This is the essential operation. It is not sufficient to read about it. Practice must go alongside the reading (Fig. 87).

Figure 88. Figure-of-eight: stage 6

Figure 90. Right side of a grafted seam

Figure 89. Figure-of-eight: stage 7

Figure 91. Wrong side of a grafted seam

6. Leave the bottom half of the figure-of-eight on the first needle. Do not release. Hook the top half loop of the figure-of-eight onto the second needle. Leave the sections of the figure-of-eight all along the row and do not release until the end of the graft. Incidentally, the top half of the figure-of-eight can be taken underneath the needle before being deposited on to the next needle. Find out which method suits you best (Fig. 88).

7. Repeat the process. Knit off the top half of the figure-of-eight to make a slack enough loop. You can draw up the yarn more tightly in the process of transfer (Fig. 89).

8. These illustrations (Figs 90 and 91) show the right and wrong sides of the grafted seams. At the end, break the yarn and pull it through the last loop. Lift all the loops off the needles. The graft is complete.

Hints and tips

1. If you need the machine before you have finished the graft, lift off all the completed loops. Hold the last

one with yarn attached, with a safety pin. When you come to resume the graft, hitch up a few loops to distribute the weight and hang onto the needles those stitches or loops you have not grafted, and repeat the process.

2. The second lot of stitches can be pulled through and left hanging on the one set nearest to the machine (one stitch per needle). This gives a tight, clean finish and is ideal for seams and for the application of bands and braids. There is no better linking method for braids than the figure-of-eight graft. It is also excellent for seaming the two sections of a circular yoke; yoke sections made on the machine need to be seamed invisibly, with economy and without bulk.

3. The needles can be pushed out to HP. This means that the approach from the back is a long armed one across to the extended needle, which is pushed back as the bottom half of the figure-of-eight is caught by the hook. Expert knitters can do this very quickly indeed.

4. The figure-of-eight graft is a good method to

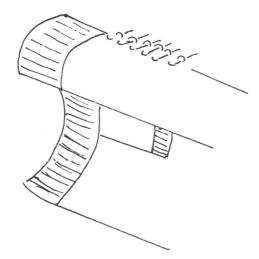

Figure 92(a). Securing a pre-knitted patch pocket

Figure 92(b). Cardigan fronts with two patch pockets

use in securing the side of a pre-knitted patch pocket to the main part of the garment (Fig. 92). Hold the front of the jacket sideways to the machine and pull the needles through, leaving two bars of yarn between each needle. The front piece hangs on the machine. Pick up the loops on one side of the pocket. Ease the front over the picked up loops and turn the garment over so that the loops hang over the wrong side of the front. Graft off all the pocket loops.

Alternatives to the figure-of-eight graft
I am concerned here with finishes which are as flat and neat as possible and which create a narrow joining edge.

1. The chain cast off can be accomplished in various ways. The simplest way is to knit a row on tension 10 (or 8 on the Passap) over all the hung loops that are to be sealed off. The knitter then uses the work tool to chain-cast off, or the Knitmaster linker if the machine in use is a Knitmaster. A neat chain edge is the result.

2. Method 1 has one serious disadvantage: tension 10 is not always slack enough for the task in hand. Ribber and double bed owners can use the second

Figure 93. Using the P carriage and the Knitmaster ribber to create a loose casting off row

bed. Before the last row, arrange for double bed ribbing. Set the lever to half pitch (Passap – racking handle down). Push into WP on the second bed one in three or four needles. Set the main tension to 10 and the ribber tension to 5. Knit across. Release the loops on the second bed. Knitmaster owners – use the P carriage (Fig. 93). Ease the loops into the main bed stitches. Cast them off as for method 1. Single bed owners can create their own loose tension by knitting back each stitch by hand.

3. Crochet cast-off is deservedly popular. Instead of following the directions of most manuals and slipping one stitch over the other held in the work tool latch, slip *both* behind the latch. Take a bite of yarn with the latch head jaws. Close them and slip both held stitches over the closed latch. The knitter can control the tension of this cast off by increasing the number of chain stitches between each decrease (Fig. 94). This method is as good as the figure-of-eight but, strangely enough, it is not as speedy to the practised hand. It is best kept for small areas like

shoulder seams and pockets. One of the pockets illustrated in Figure 92(b) was completed by the crochet cast-off method, the other by the figure-of-eight. It is impossible to tell from the right side of the garment which method was employed for which pocket.

4. If you can crochet, then the two sections can be seamed using a crochet hook. This method is the most relaxed of all as it is not accomplished at the machine. It is certainly one which is popular with Japanese knitters, who appear to move between machine and hand knitting and crochet more easily than we do (Fig. 95).

Moreover, if you crochet, compare the finish with the figure-of-eight graft and you will find it hard to tell the difference. The figure-of-eight tends to be more regular and is of course, done at the very edge of the fabric.

5. Binding off is also a popular method of seaming and linking, especially with knitters in the U.S.A. (Fig. 96). Again, it occurs in most Japanese manuals. Binding off is really backstitching through the open loops of the last row in main yarn. This can be done on the machine where the work can be held taut as the

Figure 94. The crochet cast off

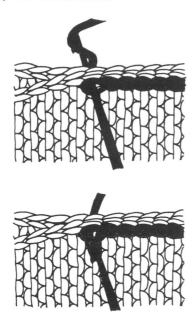

Figure 95. Crocheting a seam together

back stitches are drawn evenly through with the tapestry needle. Alternatively, the knitter can scrap off in a few rows of WY and back stitch-bind off in a more relaxed fashion. This method is ideal for use on a polo collar which has been knitted from picked up stitches round the neck; a cast-off edge on a polo collar does not look correct. It has also the effect of nipping in the collar and spoiling its shape.

Since the minimum of bulk and the maximum of neatness in the finish are a concern, mattress stitch is not under consideration. I have not mentioned the Bellinky, overlocker or sewing machine. With regard to the latter, more knitters are using it with greater skill on knitwear. Most homes have a sewing machine and it is a great pity not to use it to clear away with speed and efficiency that making-up aftermath of machine knitting.

Before you use the sewing machine, pin together the sections for seaming and overcast – baste using transparent nylon thread (the kind used for Knitmaster punch lace). This preparation uncurls the edges and facilitates the stitching up process. A medium zigzag stitch is a good stitch to use, though you can

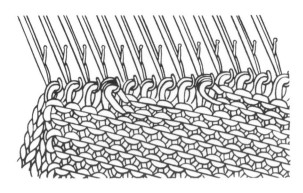

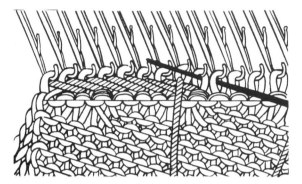

Figure 96. Binding off

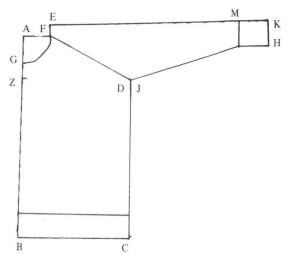

Figure 97. Block for the all-in-one raglan.

Total bust with ease	ZD × 4	=	106.5 cm (42 in)
	AZ	=	25 cm (10 in)
	AB	=	61 cm (24 in)
	AG	=	6 cm (2½ in)
	AF	=	16 cm (6 in)
	EK	=	72 cm (28 c22 in)
	HK	=	24 cm (9 in)
Welts	MK	=	6 cm (2½ in)

Figure 98. Lady's fringed raglan sweater

follow the example of many Japanese machine knitters and just use a straight stitch. In that case, the simplest sewing machine is an ideal tool. Stretch stitches, of course, provide an elasticity comparable to knitted fabric. They have a serious disadvantage in that no mistake can be easily unpicked. The knitter ends up doing a cut-and-sew repair, whether she intended or not. At the end of normal, successful sewing operations, the transparent basting thread can be removed or left where it is.

The All-in-one Raglan Pattern (Figs 97 and 98)

There is one golden rule which must be observed. The raglan diagonals on back, front and sleeves must involve identical decreases and increases. The best armhole depth of raglan which ensures this is one that measures a quarter of the actual bust or chest measurement, so for a 100 cm chest the measurement of the raglan from the armhole cut-away to the highest point must be 25 cm. If this is not deep enough for a man, adjust the stitches, add extra rows to all the diagonals and distribute the shapings evenly. A popular tension is 28 stitches – 40 rows per

100 cm. Look through your classic raglan patterns in 4-ply and you will find when you check the shapings that a great many will translate to the all-in-one method. Only one size is printed here, but at least the instructions give you a clear indication how to knit the sleeve pattern from the top downwards in an integral raglan. The skirt pattern which follows is a bonus. It is for ladies with larger figures who would hesitate before knitting a complete ensemble for themselves. The simple A-line shape has been well-tried and is deservedly very popular.

Round-neck Fringed Raglan Sweater

Size
To fit 101.5 cm (40″) chest. Actual measurement 106.5 cm (42″).

Materials
400 g (14 oz) 4-ply acrylic-nylon or equivalent. Oddments of WY in three colours.

Tension
28 sts – 40 rows per 10 cm.

14.3 cm per 40 sts. 15 cm per 60 rows.

T 7. (Passap Duo St S 6).

Machine used
Knitmaster 326.

Back
Cast on 148 sts. Arrange for 1 × 1 rib on T$\frac{2}{3}$ (Passap St S 4$\frac{1}{2}$). Knit 26 rows.

Single bed welts
Knit on T 4. 2 × 1 mock rib. 26 rows deep and 1 fold row. (RC 53). Change to stocking stitch and MT. RC 000. Knit 140 rows. Adjust.

Raglan shaping
RC 000. Carr at right. Set cam levers to hold (Passap BX and pushers). Push out to HP 2 ns opposite carr on next 2 rows, not forgetting to wrap the HP needle nearest to the first WP needle before the carr returns to prevent a hole. Push out 1 needle opp car to HP on every row for 98 rows. RC 100. Scrap off on 6 rows of WY Col 1 sts on back neck. Release carefully from the ns. Push empty ns back to NWP. Carr at right. Change to WY Col 2, push back into UWP alt needles along right raglan diagonal. Knit 6 rows and release sts carefully from ns. Push empty ns back to NWP. Carr at right. Change to WY Col 3. Push back into UWP all ns along left raglan diagonal, knit 6 rows. Release from machine.

Front
As for back to raglan shaping.

Raglan and neck shaping
As for back to T 64. Carr at right, 82 sts remain. With a length of WY threaded through a double eyed bodkin, take off centre 26 sts. Take back on the nylon cord 28 sts to NWP at extreme left (Fig. 99).

Cont on sts at right opp carr. * Push out to HP 2 sts on neck edge on next and every foll alt row, 3 times in all. Push out to HP 1 stitch on neck edge 4 times in all (10 sts held at neck edge). Cont straight at neck edge.

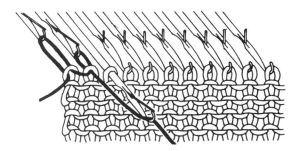

At the same time when the carr is at the left, cont to put 1 needle into HP on the raglan diagonal every alt row till all sts are held. RC 100 **.

Carr at right, change RC to 64. Bring back into WP ns held on nylon cord. Put 1 needle into HP on raglan diagonal. Knit the row. Carr at left. Work as for right part of neck as per pattern from * to ** but read left for right. Complete as for other side. RC 101.

Take carr to right over held sts. Change to WY Col 3 and scrap off as for right back diagonal. Push empty needles to NWP. Take carr to extreme left. Change to WY Col 2 and scrap off as for right. Push empty ns to NWP. Carr to left. Change to WY Col 1 and scrap off left side of neck. Do the right side the same.

Sleeve – graft knitted from the top downwards (Figs 100 and 101)
Push up 10 ns. (5 each side of 0). Cast on by e wrap. Alternatively, begin with WY T 7, knit 5 rows. Carr at left. Change to MY knit 1 row to right. With wrong side facing, top neck towards the centre of the machine, hook up all held stitches (and their wrapped loops) of back to the left of the 10 sts already on the machine. Remove WY. Take front, wrong side facing, neck towards the middle and place sts (as for back) to the right of the centre sts. Remove WY. RC 000.

Push all ns left and right of centre 10 to HP. Lift yarn between last 2 ns at HP at right. Push 1 needle at left on opp side of carr to UWP on next row. Repeat at right. Cont till 98 rows have been knitted always remembering to wrap yarn before knitting next row.

Push 2 ns to UWP on next 2 rows. RC 100 (112 sts) RC 000. Knit 6 rows, dec 1 stitch f f using 2 eyed tool at each end of 7th and every foll 7th row 22 times in all. Knit 6 rows. RC 160 (68 sts).

Cuff
Transfer for rib as for back. Knit 25 rows. Last row knit at rib tension plus 2. Bind off or crochet off loosely.

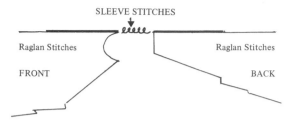

Figure 100. Preparing to knit the sleeve downwards for an all-in-one raglan

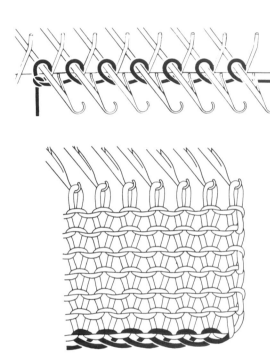

Figure 101. The 'e' wrap (top) and its cast-on edge (bottom)

Single bed owners – follow instructions as for back. Scrap off in WY. Catch first row of MY sts down on inside of cuff. Remove WY.

Do the other sleeve the same, but hook back up at the right of the centre, and front at the left.

Collar (two pieces)

Using MY cast on 94 sts using e wrap. Carr at right T7. RC 000. Knit 1 row (2 rows for second piece). Push 1 needle opp carr to HP on next and every foll alt row, 18 times altog. Do not take yarn round first inside ns in HP. Knit 1 fold row on T9. Change to T7. Knit 9 rows. RC 46. Scrap off in WY.

Knit the other piece the same, but reverse shapings and follow instructions for second part.

Making up

Join straight back edges of collar and front edges using the figure-of-eight graft. Do 1 row of double crochet (U.S. single crochet) along outside edge. Fringe with 10 cm lengths of MY (2 strands per loop). Pin collar to neck making sure centre backs are matched and point is to front. Stocking stitch graft to neck edge. Remove all WY (Fig. 102).

Join side and sleeve seams, using figure-of-eight graft for a perfect finish. Give a light press.

Notes

1. The design was inspired by one on the cover of *Modern Knitting*, December 1961. The stitch and row tensions were different in the original and the collar has been re-designed and made much larger and softer to fit in with modern tastes. Nevertheless, it was touches like this which made the old patterns so memorable. The original had $\frac{3}{4}$ sleeves, fringed pockets and a fringe round the bottom edge instead of a rib. It was accompanied by a narrow, slim-line skirt in the same yarn.

2. Sleeves knitted downwards from the top are ideal for growing children. The sleeves can be lengthened or pulled back to worn elbows, the stitches picked up and the part re-knitted. There is, however, a design problem with this kind of garment. If the yarn has a sheen on it, the sleeves can look as if they have been knitted in a yarn of a different dye lot, because yarn is given a definite directional twist in the spinning and dyeing process. It simply looks different in upside down stitches. This design is very clever. The direction of the knitting on the collar pieces provides a focal point for the eyes. Moreover, if you pair this top with a sideways knitted skirt, no one will notice which way you have knitted the sleeves.

3. When you hitch up the front and back stitches for the knitting of the sleeves, make sure you catch the wrapped loop on every needle as well as the stitch it holds. If you miss one, do not worry. It can be caught into place invisibly afterwards.

It is much easier if you do not wrap the needles in hold on the raglan diagonal. Knit as for the collar pieces. You will then get a pretty, lacy effect instead of a closed fashioned look.

4. On the Japanese machines move the claw weights up at regular intervals on the knitting which is progressing. This is to prevent stitches bouncing off the needles as the HP needles at each side increase in number. Passap knitters may also need to put a little weight on raglan edges.

5. In some yarns, the 'e' wrap cast on makes the fringe on the collar curl back and flop. The double

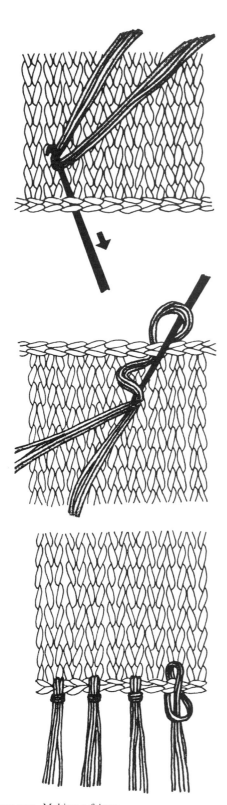

Figure 102. Making a fringe

Figure 103. Lacy raglan created by the holding position and the figure-of-eight graft

crochet (U.S. single crochet) is a corrective procedure. Alternatively, cast on ('e' wrap) over six rows of WY. Knit 6 more rows of WY, release and turn, or you can use the garter bar.

6. *Variations.* What patterns can you use on integral garments? Transfer lace cannot be done when some needles are in HP. One is bound by the discipline of the stitch and row mathematics having to be the same on all pieces. Single motifs are an obvious choice, but on the diagonals themselves some interesting variations can be worked.

(a) Knit back and front as per pattern. Knit the sleeves in the conventional way from cuff upwards and put stitches into HP on the diagonals as on the back and front. At the end, seam the diagonals with the figure-of-eight graft or crochet and remove the WY (Fig. 103). The cardigan, knitted conventionally, was seamed with the figure-of-eight graft. The method gives an attractive, lacy raglan join.

(b) Before the held stitches are scrapped off in WY and released from the machine, knit 2–4 rows in a basic Fair Isle or a weaving pattern. Alternatively, change colours for 2 rows of a 1 × 1 tuck and 2 rows of stocking stitch. Scrap off and release before hitching up again for the graft knitting of the sleeve. These touches of pattern can be echoed in a sideways

Figure 104. Holding position intarsia using two-coloured tuck and one main yarn

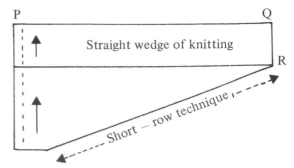

Figure 105. Section of sideways knitted skirt. There are two panels, five sections in each. Measurements: length PQ = 71 cm (28 in), waist and ease QR × 10 = 86 cm (34 in)

knitted skirt. The garment that incorporates weaving will have the purl side as the right side.

One technique hardly explored so far is using the HP intarsia method without changing the base yarn (Fig. 104). A 2-colour tuck pattern is the only indication that the stitches have been held. There is no reason why this method cannot be employed in the main part of the garment to underline the same pattern in the raglan diagonals. Incorporate stripes as well and the garment will become one of the most sophisticated.

Two-panel Sideways Knitted Skirt (Figs 105–6)

Materials
450 g (16 oz) 4-ply acrylic-nylon (hand knitting quality was used). Elastic to fit waist.

Measurements
To fit waist 81 cm (32 in). 5 cm (2 in) + 20 rows ease allowed. Wearing length – 71 cm (28 in).

Tension
28 sts – 40 rows per 10 cm. 14.2 – 15 cm per 40 sts × 60 rows. T7 Knitmaster 326 (Passap St s 6).

Figure 106. The A-line two-panelled skirt with fringed sweater

Sampler for wall hanging (Chapter 9)

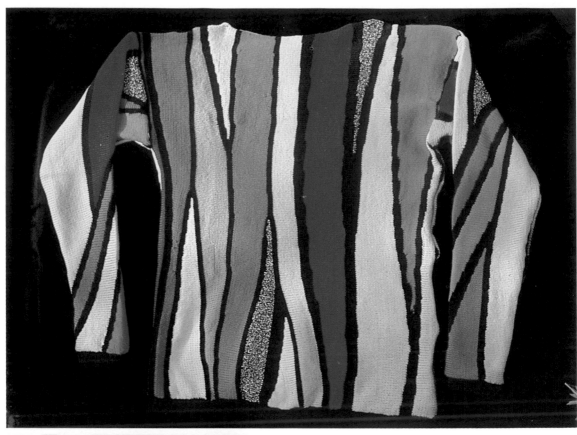

Multicoloured sweater (Chapter 9)

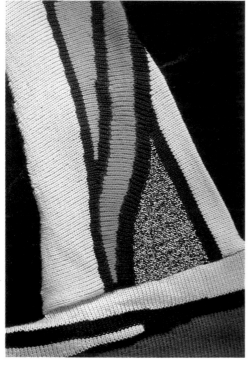

Sleeve section of the multicoloured sweater

Panel (two same)

Push out to WP 190 ns. Counting from right, push back 10th needle into NWP. Cast on with WY. Knit 7 rows. Carr at left. Change to MY and MT. RC 000. Knit 17 rows. Carr at right. Set to HP (Passap BX and pushers). *Push 25 ns at left into HP. Knit 2 rows, always remembering to wrap HP needle at left nearest to yarn. Push 15 ns to HP. Knit 2 rows. Cont pushing 15 ns to HP and knitting 2 rows. 8 times in all. 44 ns rem in WP at right. Push back groups of 15 ns into UWP on next and every alt row, 8 times in all, wrapping needle as before. Knit 1 row. Carr at right. Push back 25 ns at extreme left. Knit 2 rows ** Knit 34 rows straight (RC 87) Repeat from * to ** 4 times in all.

Knit from * to ** once. Knit 17 rows straight. RC 350. Scrap off with 7 rows in WY.

Do the second piece the same.

Making up

Seam sides with figure-of-eight graft. Remove WY. With work hook pick up bar of stitch at hem fold and crochet up in the opposite direction to the knitted rows. Begin at one of the side seams. This makes a clean cut edge fold for the hem, which should be slip stitched into place. Catch down hem for waistband. Insert elastic.

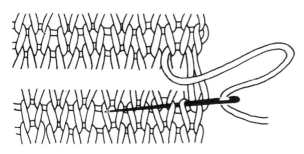

Figure 107. Using a stocking stitch graft

Notes

1. The waist measurement is created by the total of 10 wedges of straight row knitting. It is easiest to calculate the waist ease for this skirt if 5 cm are allowed first of all. The 20 extra rows occur as part of the return of the 25 HP needles to UWP. The method is to turn the waist measurement plus ease into rows and share it by 10 for a one piece skirt. Five of those groups go into one panel for a two-piece skirt.

On smaller sizes for ladies with slimmer waists the 20 rows extra ease would not be required.

2. Some knitters prefer to push 14 needles into HP and knit 1 row. Carr is at the left. They then push into HP the needle nearest to those already in HP. The needle is not wrapped in this method. Many knitters find it faster and, of course, it is a good method to use on the Passap where pushers are returned to RP to hold the needles. If a piece of hardboard cut to span 15 needles is used, then the method recommended in the pattern is the speedier. Use the hardboard piece to push out and push back groups of 15 needles.

3. There are various alternatives to try for the bottom edge. A straightforward row of double crochet (U.S. single) can be applied to the bars of yarn created by the NWP needle. Alternatively, the hem allowance can be avoided and 180 needles used instead of 190. The bottom edge must then have a row of double crochet and a row of crab stitch applied to make it firm.

4. Sideways knitted skirts in smooth yarns can drop a little after the first wash, and it is better to make them a couple of centimetres too short to begin with. This particular skirt is an excellent prototype for sideways knitted skirts. The straight row panels can be divided to give smaller wedges and more flare. A bouclé or thread can be added for stability. The skirt also looks good if two yarns are plated. One yarn is then removed in the middle of the shaping sections to give a mock pleated look. In fact, the variations on the basic theme are legion.

7 Lace – *the height of the knitter's art*

Real needlepoint and pillow lace evolved in the early sixteenth century from a synthesis of two more ancient skills – embroidery and net making. There was always an aristocratic association surrounding real lace and it inspired an almost worshipful reverence not only amongst its noble wearers but amongst those who gazed at its beauty.

It can be argued that most textile crafts are derivative. What was the original one is anyone's guess – the stitches in the fig leaf, perhaps. Each newborn craft goes through a period of being scoffed at and scorned until it makes its mark and is accepted as a genre in its own right. Lace knitting was regarded somewhat contemptuously by many bobbin and needle lace makers. Mary Thomas, in her *Book of Knitting Patterns*, is honest in showing the other side of the coin (p. 170): 'Lace knitting depicts the height of the knitter's art as it is inspired by the desire to reproduce as near as possible the art of the lace-maker.' There is usually good reason for the evolution of a derivative craft; in the case of lace and its knitted imitation the reason was obvious. Real hand-made lace was slowly and painstakingly produced, its threads so fine, its discipline so exacting as to make inevitable severe eye strain and even loss of sight; one wonders not only how much the lace ruffs of the sixteenth century cost in monetary terms, but also how much in human terms.

Towards the end of the sixteenth century, when real lace making was at its height, Mrs Montagu, a Lady of the Chamber to Queen Elizabeth I, hand knitted for her mistress a pair of silk stockings (now in the Museum at Hatfield House) in a diamond lace pattern said to have been copied from a French lace design. The pattern is 16 stitches wide and here it is adapted for the Brother Electroknit (Figs 108–111).

It is rather exhilarating to consider that the most up-to-date of machines has recovered from obscurity one of the oldest and noblest of lace knitting patterns. It could be quite a challenge to knit for oneself a pair of stockings in Queen Bess's favourite lace pattern. It was, after all, in order to imitate the hand lace knitting on gloves and mitts that the framework knitters of the eighteenth century set about producing a speedier alternative.

The eighteenth century

It is interesting that knitted lace by machine came before true lace by machine (whereby many threads, rather than just one continuous thread, were fed into the mechanism). Framework knitters moved into warp-knitted lace, which is outside the scope of this book. They were concerned, as present-day machine knitters must be, about the danger of lack of stability in single bed transfer lace. They realised that the machine knitter had not the means the hand knitter had of integrating garter stitch and purl with plain in the same row. There were other techniques that could be employed, as we are discovering; no doubt the time will come when modified ribbers will be used to introduce purl stitches to given an embossed appearance to lace (Figs 113–116).

It is equally interesting that lace knitted on the hand frame belongs to an older tradition than hand knitted Shetland lace. In 1764 an 'oilet (eyelet) hole' attachment was invented whereby stitches could be transferred much more quickly than by hand tooling on the frame. It is strange to think that it took two hundred years almost exactly to the year before a home knitting machine appeared, the Jones and Brother 585, this time made in Japan, which had as part of its equipment a lace transfer carriage. The last

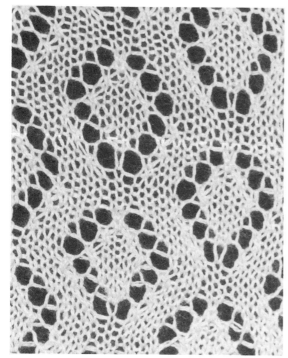

Figure 108. Mrs Montagu's pattern, sixteenth century. (Brother Electroknit)

	o		hole made by transferring stitch
	⋋		transfer right stitch to left
	⋌		transfer left stitch to right
	⋏		transfer right and left stitch to middle stitch

Figure 109. Key to Japanese symbol chart
N.B. The row that is marked by symbols and the subsequent blank row represent two rows of knitting by the main carriage.

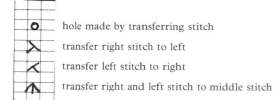

Figure 110. Symbol chart for Mrs Montagu's pattern

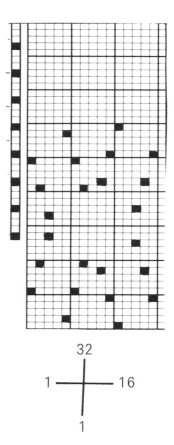

$$32$$
$$1 \dashv\vdash 16$$
$$1$$

Figure 111. Mrs Montagu's pattern marked on an Electroknit card. Data for programme

forty years of the eighteenth century were notable for the modifications made to the frame for improved lace knitting. Some fascinating, larger-than-life personalities emerge from the pages of Henson's and Felkin's histories. In the 1770s an out-of-work framework knitter, Hammond, was sitting drinking in a Nottingham alehouse when his eye chanced to fall on the hand-knitted, fashioned lace edging on his wife's cap. 'I can do that', he said to himself, and he did. By adding what were known as 'dogs' to the tickler bar (the oilet hole attachment) Hammond became the first knitter to move one stitch in one direction and then a second stitch in the opposite direction in the same row. Machine knitters call this fashioned lace and all current models of lace maker machines carry out this technique to perfection.

The nineteenth century

A century ago Victorian aristocrats consigned knitted lace, by hand or machine, to the households and wardrobes of the middle classes. A celebrated lace-maker, the Honourable Rachel Kay-Shuttleworth,

Figure 112. Shawl frame, *c.*1820. (City of Leicester Museum)

Figure 113. 1-ply mohair stole knitted on an eighteenth-century hand frame in Nottingham, 1977

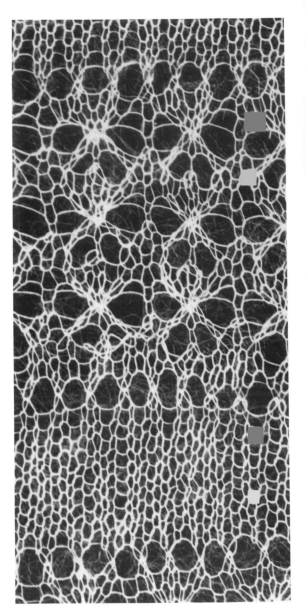

Figure 114. Section of frame-knitted stole

writing in the early decades of the twentieth century, commented in the notes accompanying a doyley with a knitted lace edging in her Gawthorpe Hall collection that such an item was used in middle and upper-middle class homes, 'but not in aristocratic circles'. She also confessed, on a ticket attached to a knitted lace collar, that she couldn't imagine how anyone would want to wear *knitted* lace. Such a view did not prevent earlier Victorian aristocrats joining with their social inferiors and indulging in the lace knitting of knick-knacks, accessories, children's garments and edgings for underwear. Moreover, knit-

76

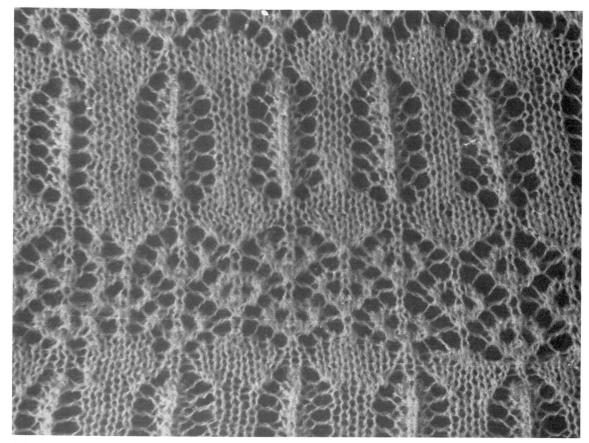

Figure 115. Two traditional framework lace patterns – the cat's face and the church window. Knitted on an eighteenth-century hand frame by Ted Dring, Ruddington Framework Museum, Nottingham

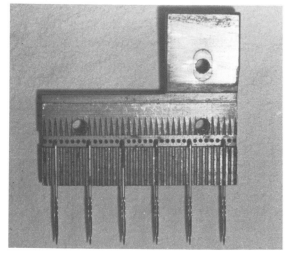

Figure 116. Section of a tickler bar for lace knitting on the frame, made by Ted Dring, Ruddington Framework Museum, Nottingham

ting – and that meant lace – was one of the few respectable money-making activities allowed to distressed gentlefolk, who had very little means of support. The romantic side of hand knitting has often been exaggerated deliberately by business interests; behind the flurry of craft activity in many Victorian households stalked the spectres of near-starvation and stark penury.

The twentieth century

A century later knitted lace may be enjoying a fashion revival, but it is looked upon with disdain by some craft knitters. Its long association with social attitudes continues, but in a slightly different context. Many craft knitters prefer the boldness of colour and the reassurance of texture to the subtlety and understatement of lace. Of all knitted fabric, lace is the most sexist. In a society that favours unisex, lace can never be anything other than ultra-feminine. What is more, the popularity of fluid, elegant knitteds, especially in lace, in Japanese fashion glossies, tells us as much about attitudes to women in Japan as ethnic knits, punk dress and blue jeans tell us about their counterparts in Western society. There is, however, a renewed interest in lace patterns now that Knitmaster has its own one-action lacemaker and now that there is an electronic machine, the Brother 910 Electroknit, capable of recovering a major part of the vast heritage of lace knitting which has been left by both hand and framework knitters. It is the vastness and the richness of this inheritance that is exciting. What is more challenging is what you do with it when you have recovered it! Mary Thomas was right: lace is the summit of the knitter's art. The planning and use of its designs, so easily produced by machine, the understanding of its construction, its contrast with space and solid, its interaction with yarn and with light, all belong to the world of the connoisseur.

The Japanese contribution

Japan's association with knitting is a remarkably short one, but as Western Europe abandoned its outdated technology and threw its archives into the dustbin, Japanese knitting authorities retrieved, collected, collated and made contributions of their own. There are so few comprehensive collections of hand-knitted lace patterns in print; industry, taught by hand knitting authorities to despise the frame, appears to have destroyed much of its unique inherit-

ance. In the 1920s redundant hand frames and their manuals were shipped from the east Midlands of England to museums in the U.S.A. and Japan. Some of the Japanese collections of lace patterns are readily available as pre-punched cards. The pattern books of Toyota, Singer (Juki) and now Knitmaster (Silver-Seiko), but especially of Brother, are rich and full and must also be a source of inspiration to handknitters as well as machine knitters. There are, however, some classics still in print. Mary Thomas's *Book of Knitting Patterns* is one. Barbara Walker's beautiful *Treasury of Knitting Patterns* (two books) can only be had in libraries. Mrs Montagu's pattern was hand knitted from the first *Treasury*. It was then put on a chart before being marked on the Brother Electroknit card. The pattern also appears in Sarah Don's *The Art of Shetland Lace*. There are smaller collections of lace patterns in other recent publications.

Symbols and charts

Mary Thomas realised as early as the 1930s the need for symbols and charts for all knitting pattern techniques, including the garment shapes and stitch patterns. The symbols and charts for lace are particularly useful. Marjorie Tillotson and James Norbury followed suit. More recently, Marianne Kinzel's use of symbols in her *Modern Lace Knitting*

Figure 117. Snowdrop lace

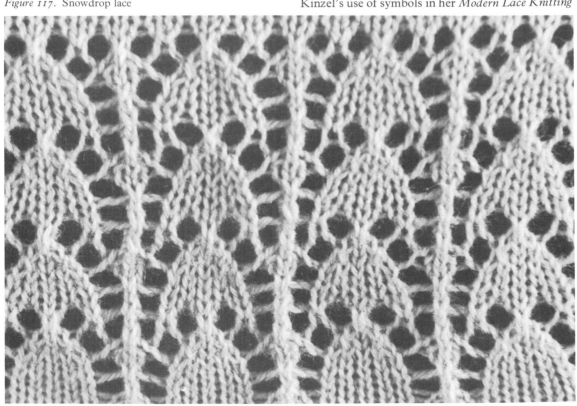

books has proved a great asset to hand knitters. Whilst it is understood that the symbols used suit each author's purpose, it is unfortunate that no-one appeared to agree on a common sign language. The system adopted by Mary Thomas, however, does show how the decreases were accomplished, and understanding these is crucial for the machine knitter bent on interpreting. The YO (yarn over) is easy. The circle representing the hole is a common symbol. The direction in which the adjacent stroke is leaning also indicates the move of the transferred stitch. When there are several moves of a stitch within a row to make fashioned lace, the machine knitter moves the stitch farthest away from the final hole first in order. All current lacemakers begin the first transfer movement of the lace carriage to the left, and the creator of lace patterns must observe the method used by his or her machine, or else confusion will result. This applies particularly to Toyota 901 owners.

It was Marjorie Tillotson, in her *Complete Knitting Book* who employed the simplified system which suits machine knitted lace to perfection, and which was later developed by the Japanese in the early 1960s into the international code recognised and used by machine knitters throughout the world. It is useful, but not necessary, to hand-knit lace patterns first. Choose patterns in which alternate rows are straightforward purl. Then translate them to a diagram before putting them on a punch card or pattern card. The French pattern, Snowdrop Lace, was done in this way (Figs 117–119). If you find the written instructions for a hand knit lace too difficult to follow, then look first for the YO (hole). You then must decide how the decreases are made and which way they lean. They soon make sense or nonsense on a chart. One thing is sure: the lean of the stroke must be away from the hole and not towards it.

Practice method

To try out on your machine, lock the card on a blank row of one of your lace cards, or use a piece of blank card. Electroknit owners should programme a blank

area into their computer panel. It is advisable for Knitmaster owners to treat the majority of translations as fashioned lace. The Toyota 901 machine throws the stitch backwards not forwards as on the Brother and Knitmaster machine. The lace carriage procedure is identical to the Brother, but the symbols representing stitches moved to the right must be acted on first. (UWP is D position on the Toyota) (Figs 120, 121, 122).

Knitmaster 260–360, Brother 820–30–40, 881, Electroknit 910 owners – push out to UWP (Knitmaster C position, Brother D position) the needles whose stitches must be transferred to the left. Begin to hand select from the left side of the chart at the left side of the needle bed. This is the direction you would hand knit a lace pattern row. See that the needles are aligned correctly to avoid any transfer muddle. Move the carriage to the left and you will see

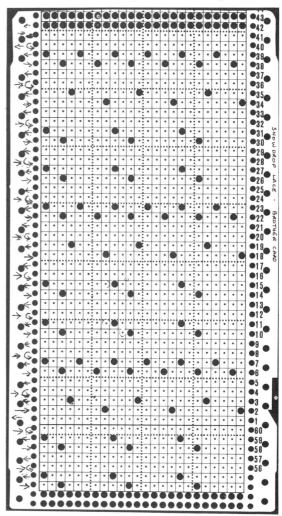

Figure 119. Punchcard for Snowdrop lace

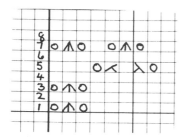

Figure 118. Symbol chart for Snowdrop lace

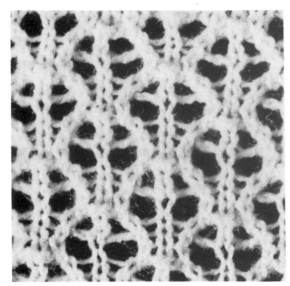

Figure 120. Lace pattern, Toyota card 19

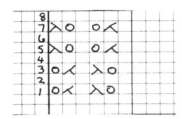

Figure 121. Symbol chart for Toyota card 19

that the stitches on the hand selected needles have transferred. Now do the same to the right, following the procedure laid down in your manual. When all moves have been accomplished, knit two rows with the main carriage (Brother and Toyota). Knitmaster owners – insert the yarn into the lace carriage, cam lever back to stocking stitch and knit two rows. If all moves within the row are in one direction, Knitmaster owners can employ the simple lace method, which is unique to their machine. The carriage selects, transfers and knits the row in one action (Fig. 123). Since the majority of lace patterns are only completed by two rows of knitting, the Knitmaster owner needs to study the pattern carefully to decide whether the next row will be plain, or will contain transfers of stitches adjacent to those dealt with in the previous row.

Once the system has been worked through and tried, the machine knitter shouldn't find it too difficult to invent original lace patterns. Since the holes punched on lace cards often confuse the knitter who expects the pattern to be delineated as clearly as

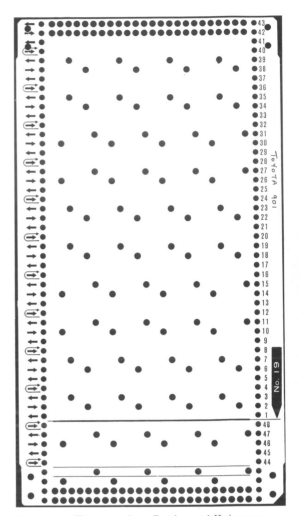

Figure 122. Toyota card 19. Brother and Knitmaster owners – copy card on the reverse side of a blank card. Knitmaster – begin first with two blank rows

for Fair Isle, by far the easiest way is to use the symbols and the chart.

How the Lace Cards Work

1. Brother

The first line of the card begins seven rows down. This line is locked in the machine as a pre-select row. The lace carriage moves to the right. Selection is made and the card is released. The lace carriage moves to the left, and so on. The transfer sequence is complete when no more needles are selected. The lace carriage moves back to the left to rest on the rail. The main carriage, set to NL (not the patterning KC setting) knits two rows. These rows are not rep-

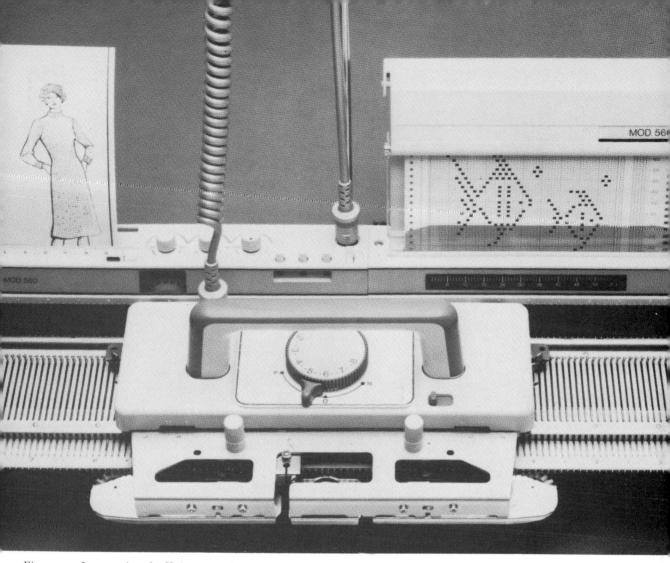

Figure 123. Lace carriage for Knitmaster 560
(Electronic)

resented on the card by punched or unpunched rows.
The curly arrow is the indication that the knit
carriage must be used for a double row. The next
move is the lace carriage. This is a pre-selection only
for the subsequent row. This pre-select row is
represented by a blank row on the card. In the same
way, the last transfer row of a sequence is represented
by a blank row on the card. There are usually two
blank rows on most Brother cards separating transfer
sequences and representing pre-select, resting or
returning rows of the lace carriage. A similar system
is employed on the Electroknit. The curly arrow is
replaced by a black square in the extreme left hand
column (Fig. 124).

2. Knitmaster

Knitmaster divides its lace into two sections: Simple

Figure 124. Brother lace carriage

and fashion (more appropriately described as
fashioned).

Simple lace

This process provides a new, speedier breakthrough
as far as lacemaking and domestic machine knitting
are concerned. The lace carriage selects transfers and
knits in one row, but it must be said that this method
can only be employed when all the stitches on one

row are moved to the left or the right. Nevertheless, some very interesting and pretty patterns are possible by moving adjacent stitches in the opposite direction in the next row, or even in the same direction for several rows before the change is made.

The first line of the Knitmaster card is five rows down and this is locked as the lace carriage moves to the right on free move slip (side levers forward). Cam lever to P to take the memory. The card is released and the carriage set to knit. The knitter merely pushes it backwards and forwards smoothly, in accordance with the direction of the arrows. The first row of a simple lace card is a punched one and patterning begins immediately.

Fashion lace

The Knitmaster machines use the same procedure as the Brother for lace patterns, where stitches must be moved in both directions in the same row. The lace carriage becomes, as with the Brother lace carriage, a selecting and transferring vehicle. It performs its function when the cam lever is set to P, when the yarn is removed in obedience to the solid red rectangles marked on the right of the card. The two unmarked rows on the card represent two plain rows to be knitted. The lace carriage reverts to a knit carriage. The yarn is inserted and the cam lever set back to 0 (stocking stitch).

The fashion lace card begins with two knit rows represented by blank unpunched areas. This is often the only difference between the way a Knitmaster and a Brother or Toyota fashioned lace card is punched.

3. Toyota 901

This machine follows the Brother in principle, except that the lace carriage transfers in the opposite direction.

Pattern Variation on the Card

First of all, it must be said that when the lace carriage is operated against the arrows a different pattern results. This applies to all makes of machine under discussion. If the card is turned over and the main carriage is moved from the left while the lace carriage is operated from the right on the Brother machine, the single bed colour changer can be used to make delectable scallops of colour on some lace patterns. A favourite pattern for use with the colour changer is Old Shale or Feather and Fan, No. 421 in Brother punchcard pack Vol. 9. Thirty-four moves of the lace carriage are required to complete one design unit. If Electroknit owners want to use the single bed colour

Figure 125. Knitmaster Card L 4 Eyelet lace (B side)

changer which is fixed at the left, then they must use No. 2 switch and reverse the position of the carriages as for punchcard machines. Punchcard knitters turn the card over and mark the pattern before punching.

Knitmaster owners need to get used to what happens on the A and the B sides of the card (Fig. 125). It is worth pointing out that Brother make their prepunched lace cards, so that a pattern can be knitted upside down if preferred: upside down lace is sometimes more interesting than right-side-up lace! It was tried by the old lace knitters, and we can see their experiments on some of the articles and lace samplers that survive.

Pattern interchange

Many knitters want to know how to translate lace patterns from other makes of machine for use on their own; Knitmaster owners are particularly interested in this operation. First of all, Brother and Toyota cards are interchangeable, provided that the knitter copies the pattern onto the reverse side of a blank card to ensure that the lace carriage performs the transfer process in the correct direction for the machine in use.

It will be seen from the Knitmaster version of the

Figure 126. Section of the lace pattern. Print o'the Hoof, or Fishtail, pattern

Shetland pattern, the Print o' the Hoof, or Fishtail as it is called in France, that it is identical to the Brother version (card 18 in the 881 pack, 21 in the 830–40 pack, L 10 in the Knitmaster pack). There is one notable exception. On the Knitmaster card the pattern begins with 2 blank rows and ends with 2 punched ones (Fig. 127). It is the reverse on the Brother, because of the different methods of selection already discussed (Fig. 128). The majority of Brother cards end with 2 blank rows and it is advisable for Knitmaster owners to stay with these for the purpose of translation. The direction of the arrows on the Brother card need not concern the Knitmaster owner, who must concentrate on transferring holes to a blank card. Lay the Brother card over a blank Knitmaster one, overlapping at the top with two rows of the Brother card. At the bottom you should see 2 blank rows of Knitmaster card. If you are copying from a pattern book, begin with 2 blank rows before copying the holes onto the card with pencilled rings. Finish the card with 2 punched rows. Check that 2 blank rows separate each sequence before you punch. On completion mark the row numbers at the right of

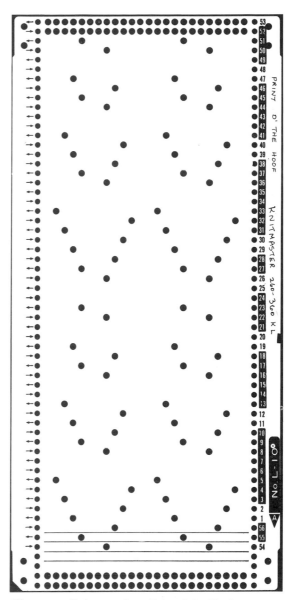

Figure 127. Knitmaster L10. Print o' the Hoof, or Fishtail, pattern

the card to show where you remove the yarn for as many transfer moves as you require. These are marked in red on fashion lace cards. Leave the numbers representing unpunched rows unmarked. Remember that your marks represent rows that are 5 clear rows down on the card. Brother and Toyota owners will reverse the process; their first row begins 7 clear rows down.

There is no reason why Knitmaster owners cannot use a Brother or Toyota card as it is. First mark the numbers on the right of the card, as for all Knitmas-

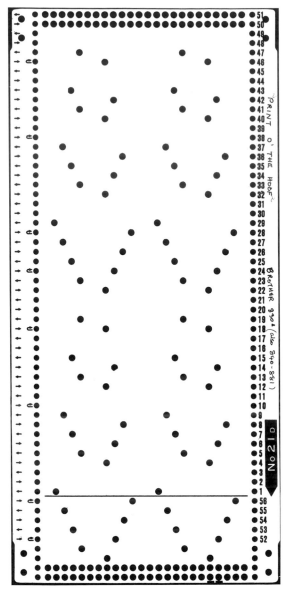

Figure within: right side vertical text reads "PRINT O' THE HOOF", "BROTHER 890' (also 840-881)", "No 210 D"

Row numbers on right: 51, 50, 49, 48, 47, 46, 45, 44, 43, 42, 41, 40, 39, 38, 37, 36, 35, 34, 33, 32, 31, 30, 29, 28, 27, 26, 25, 24, 23, 22, 21, 20, 19, 18, 17, 16, 15, 14, 13, 12, 11, 10, 9, 8, 7, 6, 5, 4, 3, 2, 1, 56, 55, 54, 53, 52

Figure 128. Brother card 21 (830–40) or card 18 (881). Print o' the Hoof, or Fishtail, pattern

ter fashion lace cards. Insert the card and lock it 4 rows below the first row as it is marked for the Brother or Toyota user. This ensures that the first two rows will be the knit rows represented by blank unmarked areas at the top of the Brother or Toyota cards.

Knitmaster simple lace for the Brother or Toyota machine

There may be occasions when the Brother or Toyota owner may wish to follow the Knitmaster simple lace technique. Brother owners should put a Knitmaster simple lace card A side up in the machine. Lock it on row 3, your first row, which is 7 rows down. Place the lace carriage at the left. Toyota owners should use the B side of the card and follow the arrows, starting with the lace carriage at the left. Select to the right, release the card and then transfer to the left. Now set your main carriage to KC Brother (punchcard machines only), or side levers to C (Toyota 901). Knit the row; the needles will stay selected, but the card will not move on. Lift the lace carriage over the knit carriage and repeat the process. You are following the arrows and are creating Knitmaster simple lace. Brother 881 owners need to put the first needle selection cams out of action before they start, or else they will be pushing back the first and end needles on every row.

It won't take long to realise that many Knitmaster simple lace patterns can be re-designed for the Brother or Toyota normal method to produce a pattern that is at least similar if not identical, but if you get deeply involved with the intricacies of lace knitting, you will be glad you learnt this method for I have only scratched the surface of a group of patterns that are noted for variety, diversity and contrast.

Types of Single Bed Transfer Lace Patterns

(1) The great majority of machine knitted lace patterns are built round slightly hexagonal shaped holes that are separated from each other by a faggot stitch, i.e. two strands from the previous two rows knitted over a hole, pulled in transfer to an adjacent stitch and crossed in a single link. The faggot stitch delineates a lacy hole and can only do so if it is pulled in the direction of the lace holes in the pattern. If the same group of stitches are selected and transferred in a series of rows the holes appear even lacier. Moreover, the adjacent areas of solid are pulled in the direction of transfer. This needs to be corrected by a series of transfers pulling the other way or else there will be bias in the fabric. The contrast of solid with hole and different directional sway is one method of creating interesting lace fabric.

(2) When the lace carriage is meant to create faggot stitch and it is operated in the opposite direction to the arrows, it creates instead almond-shaped eyelet stitches. The fabric looks as if the areas of solid have been punctured by slits. A chunkier fabric is the result because the transfer goes against the grain and directional line of holes, and half closes the hole with the bulk of stitch it hauls down with it. If Knitmaster owners try any of their simple lace cards on the B side by accident, and operate the

carriage from the left as for the A side, eyelet lace will result. Similarly a Brother owner using a Toyota card on the Toyota right side will get eyelet lace. Electroknit owners should use No. 2 switch for reversal.

(3) In Knitmaster simple lace the areas of solid are smoothed off at the sides, providing a strong contrast with the lace pattern, which is formed either by open faggot stitches or by what looks like a zigzag trellis of bars. In lace terms this is referred to as herringbone faggot. The bars are crossed, but at the junction of bar with solid. Knitmaster owners might like to try an experiment with basic card 1 (not the lace card) and knit it as a simple lace card (Fig. 129). A stretchy herringbone lace is created which is ideal for collars and cuffs. It is this which forms the lace background for many simple lace cards. It can also occur in Brother and Toyota lace as it depends very much on where the transfers are made.

(4) In some of the earlier pattern books, notably the *Brother 585–8* stitch pattern book and *Toyota Knitting Patterns*, there appears a small but very interesting group of lace patterns which we can call fashioned herringbone lace. Like the simple Knitmaster herringbone lace, only one knit row instead of two separates the transfer sequences but, unlike the Knitmaster version, transfer takes place in both directions on every row. If one examines the lace bars one recognises eyelet, conventional faggot, herringbone and single strand links. This version is perhaps the most intriguing and beautiful of all.

Mixing the lace

Referring back to those early manuals one realises that the loveliest lace is often created by mixing the

Figure 129. Knitmaster basic card 1 (herringbone lace)

methods. In fashioned and simple herringbone lace stability can be a problem, especially in the latter. In the former the most successful laces are where the swing of the transferred stitches is carefully worked out. Interest is created by stitch shunting and the many moves of the carriage. There is always good contrast between solid and space, spanned by a delicate cobweb of tracery. Our Regency and Victorian forebears did a lot of this intricate hand-knitted lace in their whitework knitting. Our collections of lace patterns will show that this complex and sophisticated fabric involves the purl row in the patterning as well as the knit and this is why, on the machine, only one knit row separates the transfer sequences. The yarn must be strong with a good twist because of the one strand situation. The Japanese symbol diagram helps enormously in the card-planning. It means however, switching from simple to fashioned lace (Knitmaster) and involves the use of the main carriage set to patterning (Brother and Toyota). The lace carriage has to be lifted over the main carriage, and that can prove tricky if you have not studied where and how it fits on the rails. Like everything else, you learn a programme and follow it.

There are, of course, more straightforward ways of creating contrast. One very interesting stitch is Bird's Eye Shetland mesh, No. 173 in Vo. 3 of the *Brother Stitch Pattern Book*. It is interesting because two adjacent needles are actually left empty in the transfer sequence, which helps to create a strong, clearly defined hexagonal space with textural appeal in the mesh. Organise an area of solid in the middle of the mesh as in the pattern on page 66 of Knitmaster's Pattern Collection No. 4 and a most attractive stitch is the result. On p. 10 of the same collection there is a pattern which is almost identical with the old Spanish lace called Madeira Wave. This is accomplished by the Knitmaster simple lace method of contrasting faggot stitch with the more delicate herringbone.

On the Toyota 787 – an earlier model of lace maker in which the main carriage selected as well as knitted the row, while the lace carriage transferred – I once created an eyelet lace in which the textural contrast was highlighted by making the same needles select for two consecutive rows (Figs 130 and 131). This had the effect of throwing delicate lace holes against crunchy almond-shaped slits; the appearance on the garment was bold and very pretty.

Perhaps one of the most subtle and fascinating laces emerges as the result of pulling faggot stitches first one way and then the other. It need only happen a couple of times in a sequence to give a pattern a real lift. The attractiveness of the snowdrop lace lies with the needles that are selected twice in consecutive

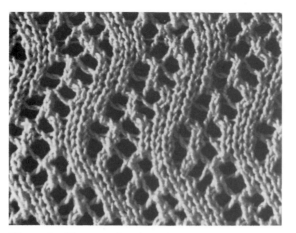

Figure 130. Toyota eyelet zigzag lace (787)

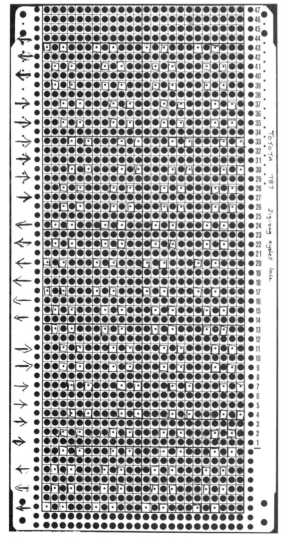

Figure 131. Toyota lace card for the 787

sequences, but their stitches are pulled in opposite ways. It is worth pointing out to Brother owners who have the choice of tuck, weave and fine lace to contrast with normal lace that, as far as fine lace is concerned, they need to choose simple patterns with a few moves of the lace carriage. In fine lace only half the stitch is pulled onto an adjacent needle. If there are too many moves of the lace carriage the half-pulled stitches pile up and a muddle ensues.

Finally, with the introduction of up to 60 stitch repeats on the Brother Electroknit machine there will be even greater possibilities of variety and contrast, not only with fashioned lace, but with solid on mesh (Fig. 132). Knitters will be much freer to explore the potential of a large stitch base repeat.

Yarn and Lace

Yarns matter enormously in the creation of a lace. Quite often you choose a yarn and a lace pattern only to find the one does not like the other. Generally speaking, brushed yarns are best used with simple lace patterns and strong smooth yarns show fashioned lace off to perfection. What's more, when a pattern involves stitch shunting, it is obvious that the yarn should be strong. These are the yarns which show off to advantage the texture of a swing. Though the machine knitter cannot introduce garter stitches, a purl with plain in the row, it will be obvious to anyone who handknits a lace and then compares it with the machine knit version that the latter is firmer, shows much more clearly the line of a swing and produces more interesting bumps and protrusions over multiple decreases. Additionally, if a silky yarn is used (and bright acrylic is very successful), the light is reflected from the surface of the lace in little gleaming flakes, which add another dimension, especially if the light glances off the swinging curves of a pattern in a myriad different directions.

Obviously, the finer and daintier the yarn the more expensive-looking and exclusive the lace that results. Pure silk is beyond the reach of most of us, but that is the ultimate in yarn choice. However, there are fine, firm, pure wools which produce laces which can indeed be pulled through a wedding ring (Fig. 133). Cotton is another choice which is traditional, especially in white for household articles, but there is a limit to the number of acceptable items one can knit for the modern home. Cotton is a favourite for lightweight wear. A lacy cotton top is most comfortable in the heat of summer. Don't forget that many of the branded 2- and 3-ply synthetic yarns on cone produce lovely lace fabrics suitable for many purposes.

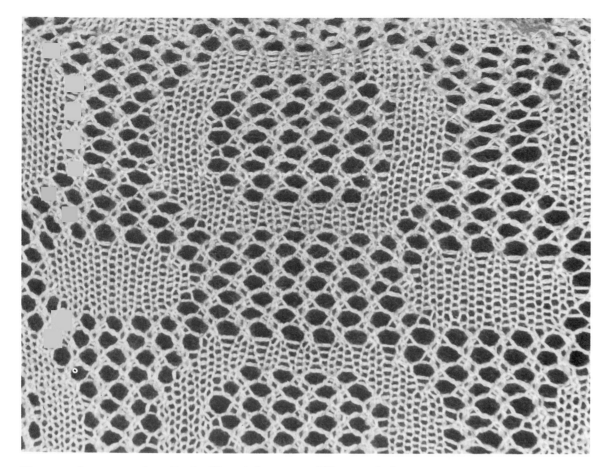

Figure 132. Lace pattern 8–30, Brother Electroknit

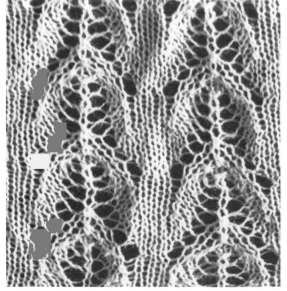

Figure 133. Chevron lace. Brother pattern No. 424, prepunched cards Vol. 9

Hints and tips

A new knitter tends to push the carriage down, not across. A light, firm and regular action is required to operate the lace carriage. No lace knitter should attempt to go too fast. The transferring needles must be given time not only to ride the transfer platform and deposit the stitch onto the adjacent needle, but also to relax back into position again. The Knitmaster knit-lace carriage must pass the pattern panel by at least 5 cm. It must not be returned with a jerk. Dropped stitches can be a headache to a new knitter. There can be many causes, including those already mentioned. The reason could also be one of the following:

1. The yarn is not suitable for the lace pattern.

2. The stitch and yarn brake tensions are too tight or too loose. As a general rule, the stitch tension for lace should be from a point to one whole number tighter than stocking stitch. On fashioned lace the tension should be about the same as stocking stitch. Knitmaster fashioned lace knitters should tighten the yarn brake tension to 4 or 5. As the yarn tends to take up slack as you are inserting it for the 2 knit rows give

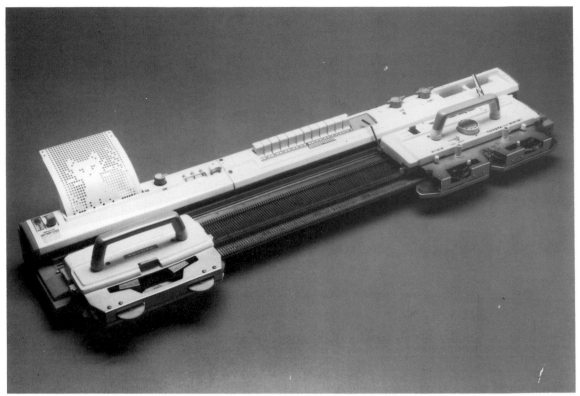

Figure 134. Toyota 787 (Aisin U.K.)

the yarn a gentle tug down at the back of the yarn mast.

3. The yarn needs a little wax or the squirt of a wax spray to flatten the hairs. If the yarn is a brushed yarn, it will not be appropriate to flatten the hairs, but it may well not be a suitable lace yarn. Brother and Toyota knitters should put the wax rings in place on the yarn mast. A wax ring may be tied to the horizontal bar of the Knitmaster yarn mast and the yarn made to pass underneath it.

4. The fabric is not weighted properly. Too much weight is as bad as too little. Knitmaster knitters should use the lace hook bars and claw weights if necessary, and move them up at regular intervals. Remove the ribber weights. Leave the comb in place and lift the fabric over the front of the ribber. If there is a tendency on Brother machines for an occasional stitch drop on fashioned lace, the latter procedure could cure it. Brother and Toyota knitters – use the casting on comb. Move it up at intervals and weight it with claw weights. The Knitmaster hanger combs, bought as a separate accessory, are ideal for all lace makers.

5. Check the machine regularly for bent needles and bent latches, and look across the sinker pins to see that they are all in line. Bend them back into place if necessary.

6. Knitters sometimes forget that lace carriages need oil. In fact, all moving metal parts require cleaning with surgical spirit, and a few spots of oil should be applied regularly. Put a little oil on a clean cloth and wipe it across the little black metal transfer platforms and across the bar on which the Knitmaster feed glides. Do the same on the Brother and the Toyota lace carriages. If the Toyota carriage rides too high and slices stitches, put a little pressure on the front part till it acts correctly. Wipe all needle butts with a clean oily cloth. Insert the toothpick end of the workhook into the Brother selector belt. Pull it out and round with a clean cloth held lightly over it. You will be surprised at the dirt on the cloth. Oil in the same way with a moistened clean cloth. On the Toyota and Brother machines the selector plates for the punchcard pattern are in the bed. Over-oiling is the way to trouble; use an oil bottle with a brush in the neck for a controlled flow.

7. The Brother main and lace carriage of the 881 and Electronic are equipped with rubber wheels which are not only deterrents to tangling, but also help to reduce the static electricity that builds up sometimes between synthetic yarns and metal – certainly one cause of dropped stitches. It can make a

88

Figure 135. Baby's layette in simple lace (Knitmaster)

muddle of a Knitmaster punch lace pattern by causing the main yarn to drag in the synthetic thread and knit it as one. To break the attraction, stick a tiny piece of self-adhesive on the fine edge of the metal separating wall in the yarn feed.

Correcting mistakes in lace

When you are correcting mistakes in lace, pull back row by row and return the stitches to the empty needles from which they came. Turn back the punchcard one row at a time and lock it. The grey touch levers in the Knitmaster will guide you to the needles selected for the whole or part of the row. On the Brother and Toyota, select with the lace carriage if you have difficulty determining which lot of stitches to convert first. If you are hopelessly lost, don't panic. Lift the fabric off the machine, wind it back and start again. No lace maker on the market allows the needles to come to HP. The transfer mechanism would be damaged by protruding needle stems. Therefore, if you wish to hold, draw back the stitches to A position on the nylon ravel cord. If, however the transferring needles get locked in a clinch, do not force the carriage (Fig. 136). Follow the instruction in your manual and gently free the

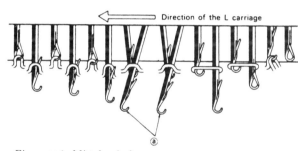

Figure 136. Mistakes in lace

needles. Knitmaster owners should remove the brush assembly unit first and lift up the lace carriage over and away from the muddle. The Toyota and Brother lace carriages can also be released and lifted off.

The Garment Pattern

Lace was not used as an allover pattern for jumpers until the 1930s. Previously, it featured on ladies' underwear and negligés and, no doubt, the first lace jumper caused quite a sensation. Lace shawls, of course, established themselves as an accessory very early on in the nineteenth century. In pattern collections of the 1930s, '40s and '50s, one can see that lacy stitches were nearly as popular as textured ones and Fair Isle.

The garment shapes were mainly classic, but just occasionally one comes across a more flowing style in neck frills, cap sleeves and softly gathered yokes. The garment shape here follows a tradition of classic cap-sleeve blouses or shells. These have been popular for summer wear since the 1940s. The garment is one of the easiest and speediest to knit so that concentration can be given to the production of fashioned lace. The shape itself was evolved from the fitted sleeve and dropped shoulder line block. The neckline was carved away and the shoulder line extended to make the cap sleeve. The curve of the print o' the hoof pattern is echoed in the unbroken garment line. The yarn is a firm, soft acrylic nylon 3-ply on cone in a delicate shade of green.

Cap-sleeved Lace Blouse

Measurements
To fit size 91.5 cm (36″) bust.

Materials
175 g (8 oz) 3-ply acrylic/nylon on cone.

Tension
29 sts – 42 rows per 10 cm.
13.7 cm per 40 sts – 14.2 cm per 60 rows.
T5

Machine used
Brother 881.
Card 18, Brother 881.
Card 21, Brother 830–40.
Card L 10 Knitmaster 260–360 KL.
Toyota 901 owners – copy the Brother card onto the reverse side of a blank punchcard. Use on the right side.

Back

For machines with ribbing attachments.
Cast on 140 sts. Knit 28 rows in 1 × 1 rib on T$\frac{2}{2}$.

Single bed machines
Arrange for 2 × 1 mock rib. Knit 28 rows depth of welt on T.3. RC 57, including 1 fold row on T7.

Change to stocking stitch and lace pattern T5. RC 000. Inc 1 stitch at each end of next row (142 sts). Knit 110 rows to armhole. Adjust.

Cap sleeves
Inc 1 stitch at beg of next 12 rows. COBH 'e' wrap, 2 stitches at beg of next 2 rows. RC 124 (158 sts). *

90

Figure 137. Cap-sleeved lace blouse

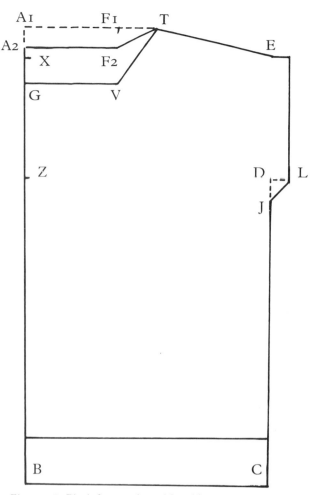

Figure 138. Block for cap-sleeved lace blouse

A2–B	= 57 cm (22½ in)
Total bust with ease	= 96 cm (38 in)
BC	= 24 cm (9½ in)
Welt	= 6 cm (2½ in)
XZ = ED	= 19 cm 7½ in)
DJ = DL	= 2.5 cm (1 in)
AF = GV	= 7.5 cm (3 in)
A1 – T straight	= 13 cm (5¼ in)
A2G	= 3 cm (1½ in)
XE	= 2.5 cm below A2

Cont knitting straight to row 204. Carr at right.

Neck
Take off onto a double-eyed bodkin threaded with WY 26 sts at either side of o (52 sts). Tie and leave. Note PC row. Using nylon cord, take back to A pos 53 sts at extreme left for left shoulder.

Right shoulder
Cont on 53 sts at right. Knit to left. Cast off 8 sts at neck side and 4 sts on next alt row. At same time, beginning at row 205 (carr at left), take back to A pos on a piece of WY or nylon cord, the foll sequences of stitches beg at far right, every alt row.

11, 11, 10, 9 sts (41 sts held for shoulder in 7 rows). Knit 1 row. Carr at left. Pull ns holding 41 sts for right shoulder into WP. Knit 2 rows in MY before scrapping off in WY.

Left shoulder
Turn RC back to 204 and punch card back to correct row. Take memory (Knitmaster). Knit as for right shoulder reading left for right when dealing with HP needles. Cont to follow the procedure for lace and always operate knit carriage from the right.

Front
As for back to *. Knit straight to R 192. Make a note of PC row. Carr at right. Take off on a double-eyed bodkin threaded with WY 23 sts on either side o (46 sts at centre). Tie and leave. Take back to A position on nylon cord 56 sts at left.

Right neck
Cont on 56 sts at right following lace pattern. Knit to left. Cast off at beg of next row and every foll alt row the foll sequence of sts (one number per alt row): 3, 3, 2, 2, 2, 1, 1, 1 (15 sts cast off in 15 rows).

Right shoulder
Beg at row 205. Carr at left and still continuing to shape neck, take back into A position on a piece of WY the foll sequences of stitches, beginning at far right every alt row: 11, 11, 10, 9, (41 sts held for shoulder in 7 rows).

Pull ns holding stitches for right shoulder into WP. Knit 2 rows in MY before scrapping off in WY.

Left shoulder

As for right shoulder reading left for right, when dealing with HP needles. Cont to follow the procedure for lace and always operate knit carriage from the right.

Front neck picot edging

Wrong side facing, pick up 25, 46 (centre) 25 sts = 96 sts. Remove WY RC 000. Change to T7. Knit 1 row, T5 Knit 1 row, T4 knit 1 row. Transfer second and every foll alt stitch for picot. Leave empty ns in WP. Change to T7, knit 1 row, T4 knit 5 rows. Pick up every alt st from the first row below. Change to T 10, knit 1 row RC 10. Chain cast off; Knitmaster owners – use linker.

Back neck picot edging

As for front, but pick up 16, 52 (centre) 16 sts = 84 sts. Remove WY *Note*: The back and front picot edges can be done as one. 180 sts to pick up. Seam up left shoulder edges first, and open out garment pieces.

Making up

Right shoulder seam: Hitch onto 41 ns, stitches for right shoulder on back, right side facing. Remove WY. Onto same ns hitch 41 sts for right shoulder on front, purl side facing, right sides together. Remove WY. Bind off 2 lots of stitches or crochet cast off, or figure-of-eight graft. Stitch tog neatly picot edges of back and front.
Left shoulder seam: as for right.

Sleeve picot edges (both same)

Open out garment pieces. With wrong side facing, pick up 53 sts either side of shoulder seam = 106 stitches. Knit picot as for front neck opening, but on last row do not pick up stitches from row below. Cast off. Stitch down by hand. Stitch up side seams and welts. No press required.

Notes

1. This is as good a pattern as any to show you how the machine deals with fashioned lace. The stitches nearest to the central ribbed ridge of the design are shunted in first. Please note that the shapings can only take place on the knit rows.

2. No lace maker allows the needles to be extended at HP, therefore, the only way to hold stitches for the shoulder is to take them back onto the nylon ravel cord, or onto a piece of WY to A position. This presents a problem because the edge needle of a holding series cannot be wrapped to close the gap between each needle group. It is not difficult to find a solution. When all 41 stitches on each shoulder piece are back on WP needles and before the knitting of 2 rows in MY, pick up the head of a stitch from the row below and place it on an adjacent needle at the side of a gap. The principle is the same as that for fully-fashioned increasing.

3. Picots make an attractive decorative edge. The one here is standard. For a more pronounced picot, leave the empty needles back in NWP for a row before pushing them forward into WP again. Compare the way the neck edge turns over onto the right side, making an attractive serrated edge, to the conventional picot finish on the sleeves (Fig. 139).

4. The Brother 881 has a built-in Knitleader. Use the datum line on the left of the plastic sheet against which to draw half the block. Another good feature the 881 shares with the Electroknit is a lace carriage

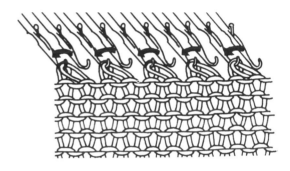

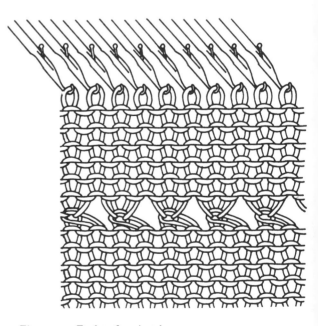

Figure 139. Eyelets for picot hem

which does not select the first and last needles. On the 820, 30–40 push back into B position the first and last needle if they are selected to prevent dropped stitches; Toyota 901 owners should do likewise. Knitmaster 260–360 owners should move the orange studs in the course of shaping so that the studs always mark the first two and last two needles, to prevent these needles being selected.

5. Electroknit owners can copy the Brother punch card holes as marks on the card. Instead of the curly arrow, mark the two knit rows by a square in the appropriate grid in the far left column. Always make allowances for the blank rows at the end of the pattern before programming the design. Providing there is plenty of space on a blank card, there is nothing to stop you using an empty vertical section to the left of a pencilled pattern as the marked column for knit rows. The empty column is not programmed into the machine. It serves only to remind you when to use the knit carriage. The first mark on the knit carriage grid column is placed a clear 13 rows up (i.e. on the 14th row) from the first row of pattern.

6. The method of knitting lace is exactly the same on the Electroknit as on all Brother machines. When the division for the neck is reached, turn the row counter back to 0, but make a note of the pattern row on the card. When the right side is completed, make a note of the number on the row counter. When you are ready to knit the left side, and this can only happen when the needles are in WP, then the row counter reading is entered and the CR key pushed. There is a built-in calculator in the machine. The rows are automatically subtracted and the pattern is ready to begin at the correct row for the division of the neck. Check with the note you have made of the pattern row at the beginning of the right side of the neck.

7. On the Knitmaster main carriage the release button makes the procedure of taking the memory a very easy one. Please note that when the carriage top is in the up position the Knitradar sheet and row counter are not clicked on but the punchcard is. The punchcard needs to be locked while the memory is taken and then released. The lace carriage, however, does not have the release button, but the P (slip) setting works in the same way. Put the cam lever to P, side levers forward and lock the card. The Knitradar block and row counter are immobilised. Take the memory by taking the carriage across and clear of the card panel and then return it to collect the yarn. In the case of fashion lace, put the side levers back, leave the cam lever at P, release the card and use the carriage as a transfer carriage until the unmarked rows appear on the right-hand side of the card.
N.B. In the pattern, the shaping takes place after the knit rows. Therefore, begin the left side of the neck by fashioning first.

8. The Knitmaster 560 Electronic machine is a lacemaker with a 60-stitch pattern repeat similar to the Brother Electroknit.

8 Ethnic and colour knitting

To the knitter 'ethnic' refers to the colour patterns of the world's romantic peasant and aristocratic cultures. The word ethnic as it is understood generally is used of any colour knitting in earthy natural colours, incorporating either the pre-Columbian designs of Central and South America, of the North American Indians, those of Kashmir of the Middle and Far East. Shetland and Fair Isle knitting is referred to as traditional and not ethnic, yet one of the dictionary meanings of ethnic is of one's own people. A better word is 'transcultural'. Even so, ethnic has broadened in meaning to cover knitting which draws its inspiration from any ancient design tradition, save that of Western Europe.

In the 1940s the Scottish scholar and artist George Bain worked hard to persuade the Design Establishment of his day to give full recognition to the rich Celtic artistic traditions of the British Isles. He did not succeed, and he has only recently received posthumous acclaim for the great work of recovery that he did. The fruits of his labour are in his book, *Celtic Art*. The Celts are just one of several forgotten peoples. The artefacts of the Angles, Saxons and Vikings lie mouldering unnoticed not only in our churchyards and museums, but in busy urban streets, passed over for patterns with seemingly more colourful association (Fig. 141). It has not always been so. George Bain pointed out how great artists of the Renaissance like Leonardo, Albrecht Dürer, and Michelangelo found great satisfaction in using Celtic patterns, which after all were from a Western European, not merely British tradition. Most important for us, the patterns appeared on wall-hangings, curtains and on the garments of great personages like Henry VIII and his even more illustrious daughter, Queen Elizabeth I.

Early Colour Knitting

The first evidence of colour in knitting was a stripe. Then the hand knitter moved to geometric shapes and, with one or two exceptions, has stayed with patterns that are easy to memorise and easy to execute on two needles. Most hand knitters would not wish to cope with the complexity of involved shapes and patterns which are not symmetrical.

The most ancient colour knitting in the world has

Figure 140. Celtic cross wall-hanging. Knitmaster 326

Figure 141. Viking interlace. Brother 840

been found in the Middle East and North Africa. After the introduction of stripes in a second colour came geometric patterns and stylised letters in Arabic incorporated in two-colour Fair Isle knitting. The latter date from the twelfth or thirteenth century and are in the collection of the Metropolitan Museum of Art in New York. The colour knitting of antiquity often incorporated symbols meaningful to the knitters who produced them. We have come a long way from that, but the longing for what our society has

lost is reflected in the popularity of ethnic colour knitting. The only knitting near at hand which gives us a sense of identity is that of Shetland and Fair Isle but, ironically, because of the doubts cast on this so-called insular tradition, that identity is more of a cosmopolitan than a national one. Surely this is the way which holds most hope for us, living in an increasingly international community. Many Shetland and Fair Isle patterns can be found in embroidery and weaving and can be traced right back all over the world to the birthplaces of civilisation itself.

Modern Machine Knitting and Single Bed Fair Isle

The punchcard home knitting machine arrived in 1971 and began to revolutionise single bed colour knitting (Fair Isle) immediately. For the first time the knitter could sit down in a comfortable chair and construct any shape of pattern providing it fitted into a 24-stitch repeat system. The procedure proved to be very simple, but completely fascinating.

1. The pattern is drawn in outline first in pencil on the graph paper that comes with the pack of cards (Knitmaster). Unfortunately, neither Brother nor Toyota supplies graph paper with blank punchcards, but it can be obtained from some dealers. Ordinary graph paper does not provide the rectangular grid which is most suitable for knitting patterns. The punch card covers repeats of 24 stitches, so usually a maximum of 23 stitches wide can be drawn on the sheet to give at least the space of a stitch between repeats. If the design is symmetrical, then the twelfth stitch becomes a pivot stitch. On either side of it, half the pattern is set back to back or front to front in the case of a reversal. If a design is set diagonally on the card, then its width can be more than 24 stitches.

2. When the knitter is satisfied with the outline, the squares on the paper that are crossed by the pencil line can be transferred to the card and punched. Some squares will be borderline cases and will be punched or left unpunched after the knitter has tried the pattern on the machine. If a hole is punched mistakenly, then one of the tiny plastic discs can be taped into place over the hole.

3. It is important when punching to hook the pin of the punch into the hole in the centre of each square representing a stitch, so that it is punched absolutely correctly. It is necessary to trim the card according to the instructions for the machine, punching two rows of holes for the overlap and two at each side for the card clips.

It will be observed from the punchcard that the vertical lines of the design are elongated. The grid on the graph paper gives a clearer indication of the proportions of the finished pattern. Moreover, vertical lines on the punchcard make a stronger impact in knitting than they do on the punchcard, while angular corners on the punchcard are rounded off in knitted stitches.

The electronic machines

The electronic machines present a more complex problem. Not only can they produce patterns which are up to 60 stitches wide, they can mirror the image, face to face or back to back. The patterns can also be

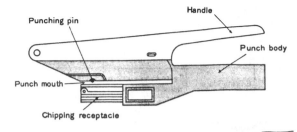

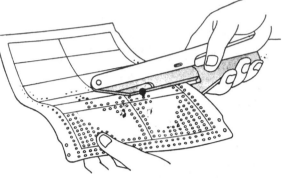

Figure 142. Knitmaster handy punch (Knitmaster)

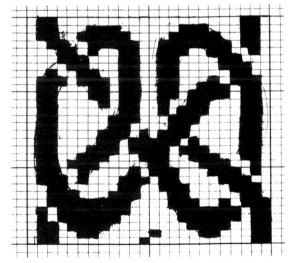

Figure 143. Pencilled Celtic knot pattern on graph paper. (Knot pattern in Fig. 140). To complete on punchcard turn pattern upside down and copy using pencilled rings

doubled up widthways and lengthways, or shifted along to a different horizontal starting position. The pattern is marked on the plastic sheet by means of a special soft pencil. Some knitters use printers ink. Brother provide graph paper and a special transparent cut-out stencil which is very helpful in the correct marking of each square. This is important, as a stray mark can give a misleading message to the computer and the pattern can be spoiled by a stitch in

96

Figure 144. Passap Deco Card 7 in bird's eye double bed jacquard

the wrong colour. The electronic machines have been with us only a short time; while most knitters appreciate that these machines excel in large patterns, very few have considered that the real breakthrough is in the area of versatility and adaptability. The real question as always is: What do you do with this pattern potential once you have understood a little how to tap it? You also need to ask how acceptable are large or multiple pattern repeats, in two colours on garments or articles you wish to wear or have about you in your home. The machines excel in the ease with which single motif and logo work can be accomplished.

The Passap Duomatic

There is now an excellent handy punch on the market for punching cards for the Deco attachment. The Deco deals with repeats of 40 stitches wide. It is worth pointing out that colour patterns on the Passap are best knitted as double bed jacquard and not as single bed Fair Isle. The proportions that appear on the card are the same as those on double bed Fair Isle knitting. Simple garment shapes should be knitted, and cut-and-sew necklines done to speed up the knitting. The Passap knitter has several types of jacquard to choose from.

Single bed Fair Isle and long floats

This is a problem, especially with the Electronic machines, where the repeats of up to 60 stitches and the expansion of up to 120 stitches can create an unsightly and uncomfortable stranding of yarn on the purl side. The answer lies partly with the knitter. Wherever possible, anticipate and organise a pattern without too much blank between the punched and the unpunched areas. If you knit commercially, you may find that strands wider than 8 or 9 stitches are not acceptable to your customers. There are other solutions:

1. The knitter can create a background of seedings using Card 1 in the basic pack as a base. Leave a space between the seedings and the pattern, or else the pattern won't emerge strongly at all. The ideal way is to make the seedings appear as part of the pattern as they do on Norwegian sweaters and jackets.

2. Some knitters cut long floats and then spend time darning in the ends for a more satisfactory result. Long floats can be crocheted up and across the purlside while the work is on the machine. Take a strand at the bottom of the pattern, twist it with the work hook and begin to crochet up. Hook the last loop onto the nearest needle.

3. One can prepare balls of neatening yarn, as for the stockings with embroidered clox, and lift the ends of the yarn up at intervals across the strands of knitting and onto the appropriate needles. The reverse side of the fabric looks as if one has used large vertical tacking stitches across the horizontal floats. This method and the previous one are ideal for acrylics that cannot be damp pressed.

4. Knitmaster have a product called yarn-bond, which is a powder that seals the floats to the main fabric. One can also buy an adhesive synthetic gauze, like Wundaweb, which can be shredded and tucked under floats. A cloth is put over the fabric and an iron applied. This adhesive material is really only successful on wool and natural fibres which can take a hot damp press. The shreds dissolve with the heat and seal the floats to the main fabric. The treatment lasts through several washes and can be repeated as necessary.

5. As the electronic machines come more to the fore knitters are turning to the double bed jacquard setting, which is as easy to use as single bed Fair Isle on their machines. A third of the WP needles on the ribber (1 in 3) are put into use. Up to 4-ply can be used as the knitting yarn. The machine is set to jacquard and a slightly ribbed fabric is the result. The advantage is that the floats are held behind a grid of 1-in-3 ribber stitches. This produces a fabric more flexible than full jacquard. After single motif work a

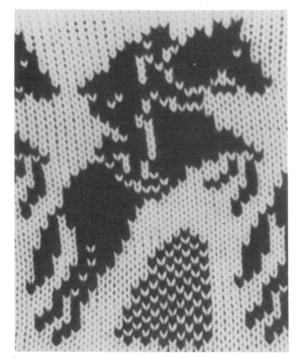

Figure 145. Horse and Rider. The fence was an addition to take care of long floats. Knitmaster 360

knitter can return to stocking stitch. This method can be followed on the Passap.

6. Finally, any patterns with unavoidable long floats should be in places on the garment where they will not be caught. Some knitters line sleeves with fine stockinette to prevent fingers catching in the strands. The best way is to leave the sleeves plain, or else to knit seedings or a vertical striped pattern to throw the main pattern into relief.

Fair Isle and Shetland

Since the former Duke of Windsor, then Prince of Wales, wore his famous Fair Isle pullover on the golf links at St Andrews in 1921, the distinctive Fair Isle patterns have enjoyed tremendous popularity.

Shetland knitting originally concerned patterns done in undyed yarns: browns, greys, off-white and natural muted oatmeal shades, whilst knitters from neighbouring Fair Isle employed subtle colouring from natural dyes on an oatmeal or grey background.

During the Second World War Norwegian refugees to the Shetland Isles brought not only yoked sweaters and cardigans, but an influx of Scandinavian patterns as well. It is now very difficult to distinguish between these and what were the original Shetland and Fair Isle patterns. Whatever arguments

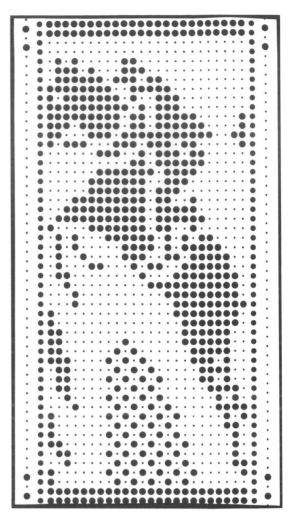

Figure 146. Horse and rider punchcard (30 stitches wide)

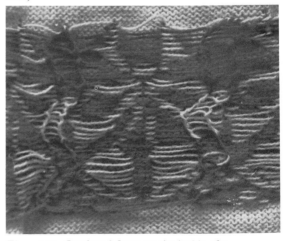

Figure 147. Crocheted floats on the inside of a Christmas stocking. Toyota 901

Figure 148 H.R.H. Edward, Prince of Wales, by St Helier Landau (City of Leeds Art Galleries and Museum Service)

there are about the supposed origins, one thing is sure: the patterns, combined with a rare skill in dealing with yarns and colours, are some of the most beautiful in the world.

There are now many sources for the patterns, some of which will fit easily into the 24-stitch repeat system. Others knitters can adapt for their purpose. After all, this is precisely what the old hand knitters did.

The traditional Fair Isle method of colour knitting

After a new knitter has mastered stocking stitch, the Fair Isle setting is the next one to be attempted. The more experienced knitter should be encouraged to move on beyond the mere reproduction of punchcard patterns in two-colour Fair Isle; time should be spent on colour interchange and in experimentation. The geometric patterns of the Fair Isle tradition are ideal for this approach, but it is not as easy as it sounds. Herein lies the skill; in the exchange one must enhance, not destroy, the outline of the main pattern. The effect must be one of harmonious unity. Wind the colours into little balls. To be authentic, one should use 2-ply jumper weight (4-ply equivalent)

Figure 149. Gentleman wearing Fair Isle pullover – Grafton Fashions, Autumn/Winter 1924–5 (Museum of Costume, Bath)

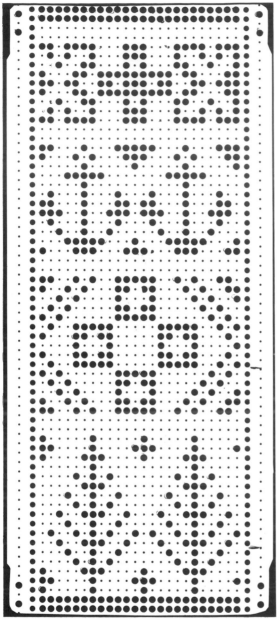

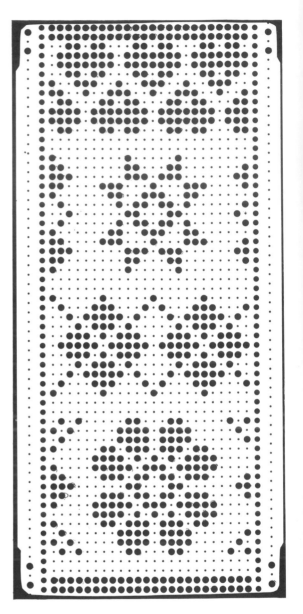

Figures 150–151. Punchcards of traditonal Fair Isle patterns (see front cover)

real Shetland wool from Shetland, and brush the pattern to blur it a little after you have finished knitting it. Oiled industrial Shetland-type wool can be used and oddments of leftover cones should be kept for the purpose. A finished garment made from oiled Shetland must, of course, be washed first, before brushing with a teasel or toothbrush, as must the tension swatch that precedes the knitting.

Place the balls in a shoe box. Pierce the lid and pass the ends of yarn through before taping down the lid of the box. When hand feeding, let the yarn trickle through your hand held just above the carriage feed. If you have a colour changer and a Knitmaster machine you can feed six colours through the yarn masts. Additional masts can be had for the Brother and Toyota machines. The Brother double bed colour changer has a four-feed yarn mast, while the single bed colour changer has a double feed yarn mast which can be clamped to the side of the machine. These aids may not be sufficient in a situation where first and second colours are changed every two-four-

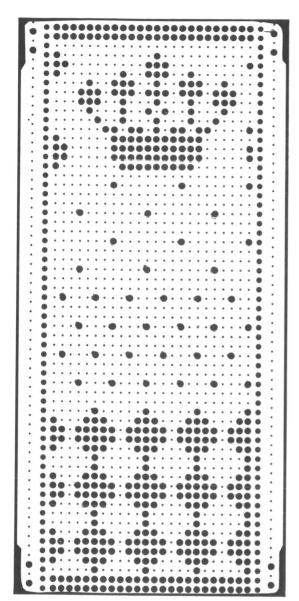

Figure 152. Punchcard for seedings and peaks

two-colour knitting, but it is, in fact, both fascinating and rewarding. It is an approach which can be used with patterns other than traditional Shetland and Fair Isle; try it with North American Indian bead-work patterns, Navajo and Maori weaving patterns and Turkish and Arabian carpet designs.

A colour and pattern experiment

The knitter's response to colour is of enormous importance, and one way of training the sense is to practise colour knitting the Shetland way. If you look through collections of patterns you will find a number that have overlapping repeatable designs, which give the illusion of three-colours-in-a-row knitting on the overlap, and a blended mutation of colours over numerous pattern repeats. If your colour sense is not all it should be, a wrong choice will break the harmony. Your task will be to find out where the odd one out fits in. It may not do so and you may have to leave that particular colour to another time. Shape also alters the impact of colour on the sense. It's a good idea to practise well before the real thing. The tiny diamond shape is an authentic Shetland pattern and you can see it in the photograph of the sample by Anneliese Taylor (Fig. 153). Sheila McGregor also discusses this pattern, known as 'peaks', in *The Complete Book of Traditional Fair Isle Knitting*, where you will find a large collection of charted patterns. Quite a few of these patterns are printed for punchcard knitting in my two *Resource Books*. Punch the pattern on an offcut of card to begin with and roll the card backwards and forwards as required. After row 3, change the background colour. After row 6, change the second colour. Continue changing one colour after 3 rows. Each colour knits 6 rows in all. Half the colours will be changed at the right side of the machine and half at the left.

A tip for dealing with ends

One thing that puts people off knitting traditional Fair Isle is coping with countless ends on the completion of the knitting. These are best dealt with at the machine. When one colour is finished, cut it down at the edge to about 4–5 cm (1½–2 in). Weave the end over and under needles 1–4. Hold it as you knit across with the next arrangement of colours. The end should now be woven in and should require no further attention at the making up stage.

Fair Isle and tension

It is a common misunderstanding that stocking stitch patterns can be used as they are for single bed Fair Isle. This is not so. Fair Isle is usually done on a tension one whole number higher. The stitches per

six rows. Occasionally in traditional Fair Isle one sees odd spots of a third colour in the middle of a pattern, which give it a special lift. This can be achieved by setting the carriage to hold and pushing out the selected needles to HP. Knit the row as two-colour Fair Isle and knit back the extended needles manu-ally with a hand-fed third colour.

There is real skill in this kind of knitting. A selection of colours may look right side by side, but knit them, exchange them and then consider what they do to the pattern before you make your final decision. The method is a lot slower than automatic

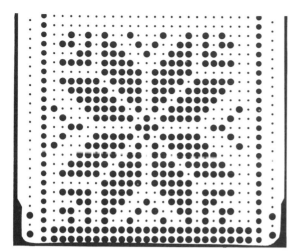

Figure 154. Shetland star or snowflake from Scandinavia

10 cm are slightly more in number than on stocking stitch for the simple reason that the strands draw in the pattern, but there are fewer rows per 10 cm. This means that when one does plain sleeves or a small patterned Fair Isle to contrast with a bolder one on back and front, there are two tension swatches to knit. A stocking stitch pattern can be adapted, but particular care must be taken to alter the number of rows for the armhole depth and to adjust the rows at the neckline correctly.

Colour, Light and Environment

In parts of the world where there are traditions of colour knitting it is interesting and useful to see what colours appeal to the knitters. Of course, people in the past were directed by their native yarns and the availability of natural dyes, but it must also be said that their environment and circumstances had a great deal to do with the colours they chose. Poor peasants tended to choose bright colours to cheer up the darkness of their lives, but there were environmental factors too. The modern Scandinavians, living in the brilliant clarity of near-Arctic conditions, choose bright primary colours or else stark black and white, as did – incidentally – the Central European knitters who produced the boldly coloured sandal socks of the last century. The Shetlanders, with their wild grey skies and seas and treeless windswept surroundings, full of the muted shades of heather, rock and peat, choose colours as soft and subtle as the objects glimmering in their land- and seascapes. What is more important, colours which look one thing under

Figure 153. Left Traditional Fair Isle – Anneliese Taylor (Oldham). Knitmaster 323

a grey, cold sky assume a quite different aspect when gazed at under a torrid sun.

Colour Knitting and Historic Ornament

The punchcard machine first made it possible to recreate virtually any realistic shape in colour knitting; the machine knitter does not need to resort to symmetrical stylisation. The representation, whatever it is, can be as realistic and as irregular in shape as possible, and this facility takes us beyond the capacity of the hand knitter into another dimension of design.

Some of the most powerful artistic symbols in Britain date from before the Norman Conquest. The designs that are most appealing are the twist and knot patterns and the grotesque and quaint monsters that seem to have haunted the day and night lives of the Celts, Vikings, Angles and Saxons. A few years ago a number of patterns drawn from these ancient sources were knitted on sweaters and sold in craft shops in two national parks in the North of England. The garments proved enormously popular with visitors and local people alike. People looked at the patterns and, somewhere deep down, there was a response, for most of the designs came not only from the local environment, but from the design roots of the British Isles and Western Europe. Moreover, it was discovered how superbly these old patterns were constructed. The punchcard designer absorbed their atmosphere and recaptured as much as possible.

Many of the designs had negative patterns as beautiful as the positive. Some designs changed their shape and their character when first and second colours were reversed. Others looked one thing when knitted as a single motif, and another when they were knitted as a repetitive pattern. Such a design was the pair of fire-breathing monsters, set face to face on the punchcard, but inspired by one inside the letter P for Plures in the eighth century Lindisfarne Gospels. As a single motif, top left on the Celtic cross-wall hanging (Fig. 140) the monsters look harmless enough, gently blowing a still-life curl of smoke. Knit them as a repeatable pattern and they release, as a negative design, a startling, disturbing Sutton Hoo-like mask which certainly was not in the punchcard designer's mind (Figs 155 and 156). This kind of unexpected occurrence does not happen with conventional geometric patterns, but it certainly helps to explain how one design can develop from another and how the carpet pages in Celtic religious manuscripts came to be covered in a seething, writhing mass of incredibly riveting patterns.

Figure 155. Lindisfarne fire breathers. Knitted pattern
Knitmaster 360

The Garment Pattern

Standing quietly in the parish church, a stone's throw
from a busy crossroads in Ilkley, Yorkshire, are three
Anglian-Danish crosses from the ninth century A.D.
On the tallest of them, as fresh and new as the day
they were carved, are two entwined animals, probably the work of an Anglian craftsman working under
instruction from a Danish Viking overlord (Figs 157
and 158).

The garment, the pattern for which is given here,
has been a favourite of many years' standing. The
long sleeveless waistcoat has established itself as a
classic garment. It is an excellent companion for
skirts and trousers, is ideal to wear under a thin coat
for added warmth and is just the thing to slip on over
a blouse or sweater. What is more, the garment shape
presents an unbroken canvas on which to display in
spectacular array ancient monsters and twist patterns. The monsters stand in arresting regular form-
ation reminding one of phalanx upon phalanx of
bestiary in a mediaeval cathedral. There is no doubt
about it, the garment is both eye-catching and

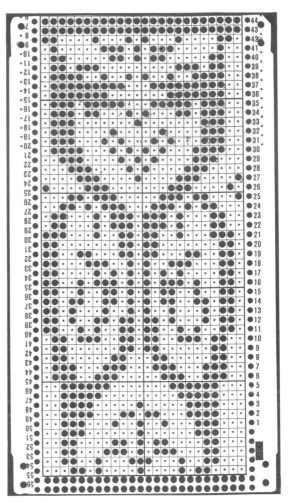

Figure 156. Punchcard. Lindisfarne fire breathers

marvellous to wear. The most interesting aspect is
that even those with the most conservative of tastes
have no objection to wearing it.

Sleeveless Fair Isle Waistcoat

Measurements
To fit 97–101 cm (38–40 in) bust. Other measurements as shown on block.

Materials
Colour 1: 175 g (6 oz).
Colour 2: 150 g (5 ozs).
$\frac{2}{14}$ oiled Shetland on cone.

Tension
32 sts – 39 rows per 10 cm.

Figure 157 Anglian–Danish Knitted Pattern. Knitmaster 326

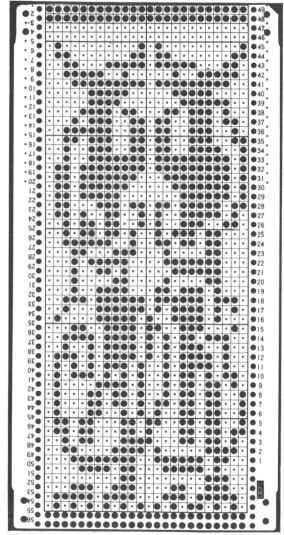

Figure 158. Punchcard for Anglian–Danish twisted animals

Figure 159. Sleeveless Fair Isle cardigan

12.5 cm per 40 sts, 15.4 cm per 60 rows on T5.2 for Fair Isle.

N.B. Wash and press swatch before measuring.

Machine used

Knitmaster 326.

Pattern

Anglian Danish design as illustrated.

Back

Using MY Col 1, COBH 172 sts. T4.2, RC 000. Knit 19 rows. T6.2, knit 1 row. Insert PC, lock on row 1. T5 knit 2 rows, RC 22, carr at right. Brother and Toyota – select on last row. RC 000 T5.2. Set to FI. Release card. Knit straight to R208. RC 000 *.

Armhole

CO 5 sts at beg of next 2 and foll 2 rows.

CO 4 sts at beg of next 2 and foll 2 rows.

CO 3 sts at beg of next 2 and foll 2 rows.

CO 2 sts at beg of next 2 and foll 2 rows.

CO 1 stitch at beg of next 2 and foll 2 rows.

RC 20 112 sts rem. Cont straight till R90. Carr at right.

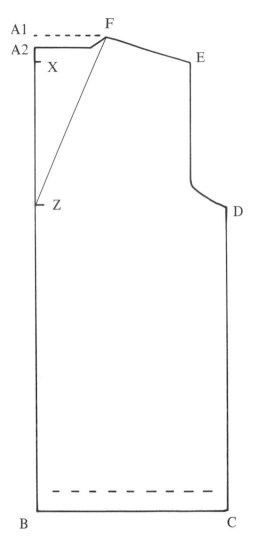

Figure 160. Block for Lady's Fair Isle waistcoat.

Total bust with ease (4 × BC)	=	104 cm (41 in)
Width of bands (not shown)	=	4 cm ($1\frac{3}{4}$ in)
Length A2–B	=	78 cm (31 in)
Shoulder depth A2–X	=	1 cm ($\frac{1}{2}$ in)
$\frac{1}{2}$ width across back X–E	=	38 cm (15 in)
Shoulder depth A1–X	=	3 cm ($1\frac{1}{4}$ in)
Armhole depth X–Z	=	24 cm ($9\frac{1}{2}$ in)

Shoulders and back neck

Cast off 4 sts 6 times at each shoulder edge (24 sts) in 12 rows. At the same time, when RC reads 94 (carr at right) take off on a double-eyed bodkin threaded with WY 19 sts either side of 0 = 38 sts for centre back neck. Using nylon cord, take back to A position stitches on 37 ns at extreme left. Note PC row. Cont to dec on right shoulder. Knit to left. Cast off 6 at beg of next row. Cast off 4 at beg of next alternate row.

Cast off 3 sts at beg of next alternate row. Knit neck side straight to end.

Left shoulder and back neck

Turn back PC to correct row. Take memory or select. Take carr to left of work. Alter RC to 94. Do left side as right side, but read left for right and vice-versa.

Right front

Cast on 86 sts. Work as for back to * (knit one extra row for left front). Carr at right. RC 000.

Armhole shaping

CO 5 sts at beg of next row and foll alt row.

CO 4 sts at beg of next row and foll alt row.

CO 3 sts at beg of next row and foll alt row.

CO 2 sts at beg of next row and foll alt row.

CO 1 stitch at beg of next row and foll alt row.

RC 20, 30 sts dec at armhole edge.

At the same time, using 2-eyed transfer tool, dec 1 stitch at left ff for V-neck on row 1 of armhole shaping and every 3rd row, 32 times in all. Knit to row 90, shaping on a V as directed. Carr at right.

Shoulder

Cast off 4 sts at beg of next and every alt row 6 times in all.

Left front

As right, but knit 1 extra row before armhole shaping (RC 209) and read left for right.

Sleeve bands (both same)

Stitch up shoulders. Open out pieces, wrong side facing. Carr at left. Pick up 70 sts either side of shoulder seam = 140 sts. Using MY, T3.2 RC 000, set cam levers to HP. Push out 1 needle opp carr on every row for 14 rows. (No need to wrap ns). Knit 1 row on T5.2. Change to T3.2. Push back 1 needle to UWP opp carr every row for 14 rows. Knit 1 row on T8. Cast off, or link off by hand.

Front band

Ribber

Near RC, cast on, full needle rib T$\frac{1}{2}$ half pitch 5, 12 sts on each bed = 24 sts. Knit till long enough to go all way round. Side weights provide adequate weight. Put sts on a safety pin at RC 900 (approx).

Single bed

Push out, near RC 49 ns to WP. Counting from right take back 25th needle to NWP. COBH over remaining 48 ns. T3. Knit until it is long enough to go all the way round (approx 870 rows). Needle in

NWP provides vertical fold. Put sts on a safety pin.

Making Up

Stitch side seams. Turn down sleeve bands and catch into place on wrong side. Turn up bottom hem and slip st to wrong side. Stitch on front band. Cast off stitches on safety pin or put back on machine to knit extra rows if not long enough. On back neck, graft side of band to stitches held in WY. Remove WY. On completion, wash garment, dry and press.

Notes

1. The colours in the original are natural brown-grey and Aran cream. The yarn is one of several kinds of oiled Shetland-type wool available in coned yarn centres or by mail order. The $\frac{2}{14}$ count is equivalent to 2-ply, but because the yarn is oiled, it is treated for tension purposes as a 3-ply. When the swatch is knitted wash it in washing soda, which is better than detergent since the oil-and-soda mix make soap and leave the fabric soft and fluffy. The completed garment is treated in the same way.

2. Quite often, sleeveless jackets and pullovers have a little extra taken off the upper front and back widths. Here the width, after shaping, is the same as the fitted sleeve block from which it came (38 cm). The reason is that the sleeve bands are narrow and curl softly over the shoulder line. This point needs to be borne in mind. Men's sleeveless garments, for example, usually have between 2–3 cm pared away at each armhole to accommodate the width of band.

3. If you wish to choose your own card you are free to do so, but each Fair Isle pattern has a different row and stitch tension. Please note that there are two rows of stocking stitch on this pattern. Remove the second colour for ease when you come to them on the card. Do not forget to insert the colour again after the two rows of stocking stitch. The cam lever stays at Fair Isle because the blank rows on the card direct the carriage to knit plain in one colour.

4. Tip for casting off in Fair Isle. At the underarms and on the shoulders use each colour alternately

Figure 161. Passap Card 19. Two-colour single-bed slip

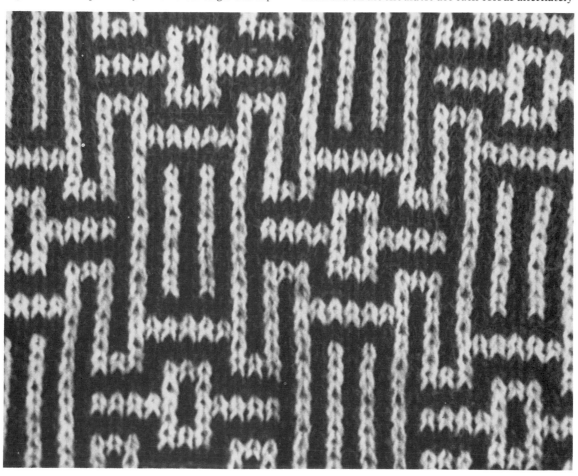

to cast off one stitch at a time. On the Knitmaster and Toyota 901 push out the end needle. Set the cam to knit it back. The extended needle always knits the patterning colour. Brother 881 and Electroknit owners can set the needle cam to select first and last needles.

5. Notice the shaping on the underarm bands. The slight V-shape is accomplished automatically by the holding position. Passap owners would use BX and pushers. The method, so easily adapted for a neckline, produces a flat, lacy, fashioned shaping which fits snugly under the armpit without the bulk of a stitched join. In the same way the fully-fashioned decrease on the V improves the appearance of the edge and makes it easier for the band to be stitched on neatly.

6. Weighted bands. The double bed casting on comb is awkward to use on narrow bands. After the zigzag row hang the two side weights and hold them down until the knitting gets underway. They may well be sufficient. If not, increase the pull down with a couple of claw weights.

7. The pattern is not written for Passap owners, but there is no reason to prevent them knitting the waistcoat in a pattern of their choice. There is nothing in the Deco manual to show the versatility of 2-colour single bed slip. Patterns alter quite radically in appearance from Fair Isle and jacquard to single bed multicoloured slip. Card 19 is a good example. The slipped stitches are held for two rows and then hauled up into the pattern sequence of the next two rows. The procedure causes some surprises. Set the machine to $\frac{GX}{BX}$ and change the colours every 2 rows. The left arrow key is down, selector dial is set to 2. You will need to do a tension swatch of course (Fig. 161).

9 Fibre art

In days gone by handloom weaving, with its associated crafts, enjoyed a unique position. As *the* textile craft in society, it supplied clothes for rich and poor alike. It was also an important representational medium: the Bayeux tapestry is a living record in embroidery of a momentous happening in the history of France and England, while the tapestries of the Middle Ages, Renaissance and Restoration provide a sumptuous cavalcade of the history and tastes of the time. The study of costume alone shows the extent to which the skills of craftsmen were employed (Fig. 162). People from the humblest and highest walks of life could see and experience the degree to which a textile craft could give value to life through both the utilitarian and aesthetic dimensions.

Knitting, say the purists, is not a textile craft. An older word than the Latin *texere*, to weave, is the Sanskrit *nahyat*, from which the word knitting is derived. Nahyat means 'net' or 'weave', and gives justification to the position knitting has assumed in recent years. It has progressed from merely providing accessories to providing garments which are essential wardrobe items. Indeed, of all textile crafts practised today only knitting can be said to come anywhere near fulfilling the role that weaving had in the past yet, sadly, in Western society it is the least represented in any celebration of textiles. Sometimes it is even distinguished by its total absence. Not so in Japan: resources are being poured into the teaching of knitting and into the training of knitwear designers and experts in hand and machine knitting. Japanese authorities recognise that the knitting field has the greatest potential of any for the fashion industry. A country, famous for centuries for its superb woven textiles, is now devoting its skills to what it sees as the material of modern life – the fluid, elastic fabric of the knitter.

Japan is certainly providing the means for people to enjoy a handicraft to the full. Underpinned by such formidable expertise from right across the community, Japan's industrial success is assured. In the U.K. it is rare to find knitting taught in state schools anymore. It is hoped that any knitting talent will be discovered in the foundation course during the first year at a College of Art and Design, and this may be the first-ever encounter a student has with the knitting craft. Nevertheless, some very exciting knitting is produced in our colleges, while at the further education level it is most encouraging to see the growth of clubs and classes in machine knitting which, as a craft, has been given honourable status by the Crafts Council.

If knitting is to assume its rightful place as the authentic textile expression of our time, it has a daunting task ahead of it. On the fibre art side, and this appears to interest Western knitters more than their Japanese counterparts, knitting has virtually no inspiration from the past, save a few pairs of gloves and stockings, an odd waistcoat or two and a handful of knitted carpets.

Definition of Fibre Art

Any definition of fibre art, or art in a craft, is bound to be inadequate and is therefore vulnerable to criticism. However, a definition needs to be given as a starting point. Fibre art is the attempt through textiles to make a statement about life. One way of doing so is to create a memorable presence, which strikes chords of recognition through pleasure, sometimes pain or even revulsion. The important point, which cannot be ignored, is that if the statement is genuine, then it ought to be recognised by sensitive,

Figure 162. Seventeenth-century Venetian knitted coat
in pale blue silk with gold and silver thread. (Victoria
and Albert Museum)

intelligent, lay people, who stand outside the idiom, the clichés and whatever is currently the in thing with the design establishment. If the statement is only understood by and made to a select few, then there is serious doubt whether the expression is fibre art at all. These remarks apply equally to machine knitters who feel their work is not understood. Their values need to be explained to those outside the pale. We are not discussing prophetic statements which will only be understood by the next generation, but works of art-craft, which should enrich contemporary life, an enrichment sorely needed in a darkening world. It cannot do so if only a few understand what it is all about.

A statement about life can only be made through the tools and materials and the craftsperson's mastery of them. There must first be the experience, but discovering the nature of materials and the means by which they can be made vehicles of expression is the way forward. Keen observation of life, of natural things and a study of other related arts-crafts are essential. What is required finally is the knowledge of a wide variety of techniques which give one mastery and freedom of movement and choice.

Pictorial effects

1. *Many-colours-in-a-row Fair Isle*

Unlike many of the great historic tapestries, the knitted carpets of the eighteenth century were not commissioned by wealthy patrons wanting to combine works of art-craft with a utilitarian purpose (Fig. 163). The carpets were, in fact, examination pieces, which may eventually have become wall-hangings, though that was not their original function. A knitted carpet had to be produced by a would-be master knitter for the exacting admission process required by the knitting guilds of Alsace and Germany. His work would be presented for judgement to the experts in his craft. (So often knitting fails to find a place in modern exhibitions because it is rejected by assessors who are ignorant of knitting values. This complaint has been voiced by Australian and New Zealand as well as by British machine knitters.)

No one knows exactly how the eighteenth century carpets were executed. It is thought they were knitted either on a peg-frame or by the use of several pairs of needles along the row. What is certain is that the knitter used a free-style, many-colours-in-a-row stranded Fair Isle, and the pattern must have been worked in mirror image if a peg-frame was used. Possibly the knitters, like mediaeval tapestry weavers before them, worked from a reflection of a chart in a mirror, so that the design would come the right way round. The work was made a little easier by the fact

that the designs were symmetrical in parts. Even so, it must have taken the knitters a long time to execute one of these carpets.

Modern machine knitters find many-colours-in-a-row Fair Isle equally slow, but very interesting nevertheless. Designs should be drawn on a large sheet of greaseproof paper, which is then turned over. The knitter proceeds to work from the reverse side or copies the design for the charting device. The charting device should be operated manually, as it will take several actions of the carriage to complete a row. The Passap Duomatic provides the exception to the rule: the pushers must be selected for 2 row runs and, as the work is on the front bed, the image on the Forma or work sheet will be the right way round. The arrow key is not used. On the punchcard and Electronic machines the card should be locked on a blank row, though the Brother carriage machines can manage without this precaution, and so can the Knitmaster carriage with side levers forward. It is a wise precaution nevertheless. The setting for many-colours-in-a-row Fair Isle is slip-part-empty, and one colour is knitted at once. The needles are pushed out to HP and the cams set to knit them back. The colour must be removed and the carriage returned to collect the next colour. Since no needles will be pushed out on the return row, the carriage will operate a free move slip.

This is not the speediest way to knit a piece. To facilitate progress, do not thread any but the most commonly used colours through the yarn mast. Prepare the yarn as was suggested in the previous chapter. Insert the colour into the carriage yarn feed and hand feed, controlling the flow with one hand as you push the carriage with the other.

If you organise your design so that for 2 rows you knit the same needles in the same colour and you have no more than 4 colours in a repetitive design, you can punch or mark a card. The holes or marks on the card will represent each colour knitted on the slip setting. This is a very useful method to use in conjunction with the more automatic punchcard method, and with hand selected Fair Isle, where a punchcard is not used. Examples of this 3 or 4-colours-in-a-row technique are to be found in Brother Knitting Pattern Volumes 2 and 3 (Fig. 164). It is suggested you use the colour changer to facilitate speedy exchange of yarns. This technique can also be worked on the Knitmaster and on the Singer. It is useful to point out that you can use the same cards for 3 or 4-colours-in-a-row jacquard with the ribber and double bed colour changer. Passap have a number of Deco Cards punched for 3 or 4-colours-in-a-row double bed jacquard.

Figure 163. Knitted carpet, Alsace (Strasbourg), 1781. (Victoria and Albert Museum)

When you become more skilful you can plan a card which incorporates three methods. Unless you pencil in the instructions at the side of the card you are in for a confusing time and a muddle in your knitting pattern. The three methods are as follows:

(a) The conventional 2-colours-in-a-row punch-card Fair Isle. (Setting: Fair Isle).

(b) Multicolour 2 row Fair Isle. (Setting: slip).

(c) Multicolour 1 row Fair Isle. (Setting: slip).

When you use (c) the card must be locked and the carriage returned free move to receive the next colour. On the Brother and the Toyota push all selected needles back into B position before you attempt to select again on a free move slip. You can use the release button method on the Knitmaster Electronic and 260–360, but the card will move on, so lock it on the latter machines. The geometric diamond pattern was planned in this way (Fig. 165).

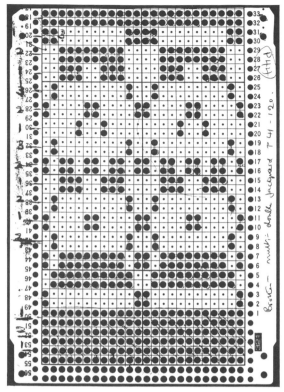

Figure 164. Punchcard for 3-colours-in-a-row Fair Isle or jacquard. (Brother Vol. 2, No. 120)

Figure 165. Punchcard Fair Isle demonstrating three methods. Helen Kinder. Knitmaster 360

There are three colours – black, grey and white.

There is a fourth method which is possible. You can knit 2-colours-in-a-row Fair Isle by hand selecting the patterning needles. Work from a chart. Lock a piece of blank card in the machine and arrange for punchcard Fair Isle. There is, of course, no limit on the width of the pattern you can select. The limiting factor is that you can only use two colours at once.

2. *Intarsia*

Intarsia is an Italian word meaning inlay. There are three main kinds of intarsia practised by machine knitters. Two of them are characterised by the non-stranding of patterning yarns across the back. In the case of intarsia knitweave, the non-stranding is on the purl right side of the work. The patterning yarns are linked at the pattern edges. In this, intarsia is different from single bed Fair Isle.

(a) *Free style intarsia*

This is a very old method indeed. It was done easily on the frame by eighteenth century knitters. It was also used by the post-Second World War knitters of the twentieth century. All simple single bed machines that are not fitted with a two colour feed can be used. The setting is stocking stitch and all colours are

laid across the row by hand before the carriage is pushed across. The Knitmaster intarsia carriage makes it possible to use this method on the modern Knitmaster machines (Fig. 166). The Corona Jumbo machine has a two-hinged feed which is very easy to use, while the Brother and Toyota current standard models have similar facilities. Picture sweaters have been very popular in recent years, but it will be observed that free-style intarsia is best used with big sweeping designs: hills, mountains, waterfalls, etc., for the simple reason that the colours must not be stranded across or a tangle of yarn ends is the result. The method is to lay across one colour at a time, overlapping at the edge, A with colour B and so on. Again, the knitter works from a chart (Fig. 167). Each end of yarn needs a little pull down to facilitate the knitting. Special little weights are available, but spring-clip plastic clothes pegs make excellent substitutes. Wind the end of yarn round the clothes peg, leaving enough yarn free to knit the stitches. Open the jaws of the clothes pegs to take a grip on the yarn and leave it. In this way, the yarn ends are organised. Use too many and the clothes pegs will be a jumble and you will end up going back to a punchcard and 2-colours-in-a-row Fair Isle. You can of course, use

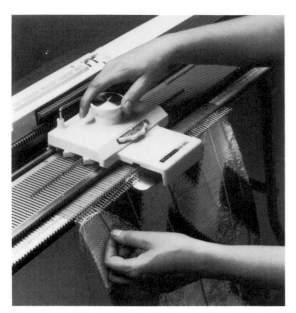

Figure 166. Knitmaster intarsia carriage (Knitmaster)

Figure 167. Chrysler coat. Susanna Lewis, New York. Machine knitting and appliqué

intarsia for main areas of colour and combine it with Swiss darning to be done on completion of the knitting.

(b) Intarsia knitweave

This method is easiest on the Brother, Singer (Juki) and Toyota machines where the patterning needles come to D or UWP. On the Knitmaster machines it is possible to do so more slowly by winding the weaving yarn in and out of extended needles and then pushing the carriage (weaving brushes down) across to knit the row.

Use a simple basic card, like card 1 in the basic pack, again following the principle of laying over. This method is very satisfying to do. The pattern comes to life in front of the eyes and is worked from a chart the right way round. The weaving yarns can either be linked or not linked at the edges. Geometric shapes are best attempted first. The knitter advances one colour across the row and withdraws the other to fewer needles. Do this with two colours first, then introduce others. There is no reason why pictures cannot be attempted. In fact, this is an underused method with much greater potential than ordinary stocking stitch intarsia. It is not likely to be attempted by handknitters, and having a distinct machine technique is always an advantage. There are excellent examples of this method in *The Book of Machine Knitting* by David Holbourne.

(c) Holding position intarsia

Early issues of *Modern Knitting* from about 1956 onwards show that this was a favourite way of introducing colour. It is certainly one which Passap knitters know well as it is often featured in the Passap Model Books. It is interesting, however, that the attractive batwing sweater from the Knitmaster 3500 manual (*c*.1953) was knitted by the free-style and not the HP intarsia method. This is because it was much easier to lay several colours across the needles of a simple machine with no automatic feed. On modern machines the batwing sweater would be knitted using the HP intarsia method.

Geometric wedges of colour can be knitted sideways or straight up a garment in the conventional manner. The principle is to push out to HP (Passap BX and pushers) the needles not required for the colour in the feed. There is a regular progression of needles involved and the HP needle nearest to the edge needle in WP is wrapped by the yarn to prevent a hole. The pattern needs to be carefully worked out, with the rows planned on a sketch and the carriage returned to the correct needles for the next colour.

3. Mixing the methods

Often the most satisfying way to produce what one

Figure 168. Brother single bed colour changer. (Brother)

requires is by a combination of several methods. One needs to master the single motif techniques as well as the two stocking stitch intarsia methods. Learn to combine single motif techniques with 2-colour free style Fair Isle, and use the punch card and single motif equipment for the centre of a design. Hand-select the rest on either side of the automatic pattern area. Free style 2-colour Fair Isle is ideal for names and knitted-in slogans. Sometimes a picture is only complete when Swiss darning, embroidery and even beads or other 3-D objects are added as well. The work of modern painters like Paul Klee, has inspiration for both pictorial and textural effects (Fig. 170).

The use of the charting device

When many methods are involved it is difficult to see how one can use the charting device. The best way is to plan out one's picture on graph paper and mark the horizontal grid as stitches and the vertical one as rows. The full scale Knitleader for Brother machines is valuable in that one can plan an actual scale, full width picture sweater. You may have to trip the sheet manually on the punchcard models but at least you will be able to see what you have accomplished as far as your picture is concerned (Fig. 171). The half-scale charting attachments (Knitradar, Forma and Pattern Driver) can be used similarly, and so indeed can the half size, full scale charting attachments (881 Knitleader, Knitcopy and Knit Tracer). The principle is to reduce the width of the block while keeping the normal scale lengthways. The full expansion of the block is used widthways.

(a) Knitradar, Forma and Pattern Driver

The widthways scale is a quarter, not a half. The normal half scale is still in operation for the rows. The stitch rulers with centre 0 are used. Use one marking on the ruler to equal two stitches, or else double up the stitch reading if there is a stitch ruler to suit.

(b) 881 Knitleader, Knit Tracer and Knitcopy

The widthways scale is half not full. Full scale is still in operation for the rows. On the 881 the centre datum line and rulers to match are the ones to use. On the Knit Tracer and Knitcopy place the block centrally, leaving equal space on either side. Make one marking on the ruler equal two stitches, or else double up the stitch reading if there is a stitch ruler to suit. With these attachments one can of course use half scale throughout, halve the row reading and set accordingly.

On all charting attachments you will get an elongated distorted block. If you copy your picture onto this from a graph showing normal proportions, following the principle of elongation, you can produce a successful picture sweater, using the laying over intarsia method. The Knitmaster Knitradar and the intarsia carriage form an excellent partnership in the production of this kind of work. The Knitradar can function in the normal automatic way.

A tension swatch using the various yarns and sampling a little of the design must be knitted. Picture sweaters are usually straightforward as far as shape is concerned (either fitted or drop shoulder line).

Figure 169. Batwing sweater with intarsia. Knitmaster
3500 manual (1953) (Knitmaster)

Figure 170. Street scene – punchcard and hand-selected Fair Isle with embroidery. Denise Musk, Bradford, Knitmaster 324

Textural effects

A common misconception is that texture has no pattern. Its appeal is to that most comforting and basic of senses – the sense of touch. In actual fact, texture has pattern, but it is irregular. An approach worth exploring is the juxtaposition of irregular with regular pattern, appealing strongly to the sense of touch in the selection of yarns and threads, as well as to the sense of sight. After all, this is a juxtaposition one can find in nature. A common household spider is one with a coal black regular chevron across a pale, primrose yellow back, edged with mottled irregular tortoiseshell sides which appeal strongly to the sense of touch in spite of their being on a spider. A knitter interested in design and design inspiration should find a magnifying glass (the kind used to enlarge small print) a great aid. If observation is crucial to a knitter, then perception of relationships is even more so.

The simplest way to produce texture is by the use of interesting yarns and threads (Fig. 188, p. 128). Go further, and make careful selection for Fair Isle. Knit leaves on trees in a green poodle yarn, ducks in a brushed acrylic, ploughed fields in a fine chenille, and so on.

There are many textures one can explore with the use of stitch patterns. It is important to consider

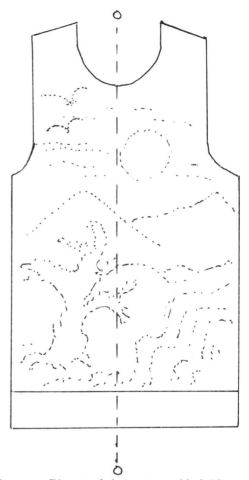

Figure 171. Diagram of picture sweater block (elongated)

more than one at a time. This approach is a far cry from the school of thought which says that a beautiful, expensive yarn of itself puts a simple garment or article into the exclusive class. To one who regards knitting as a creative medium that is not so, and the argument brings sharply into focus the clash between those with knitting and non-knitting values. It also points sadly to the fact most people regard knitting as having a purely utilitarian purpose. What I am considering here is the exploration of the nature of materials on various stitch settings, using different techniques, a prospect that is exciting a growing number of knitters.

In the sampler for a wall-hanging you will find knitweave, tuck, slip, circular cords (Fig. 173), knitted in fringes, several rows of eyelet lace as well as stocking stitch and a braided cast on applied directly over the knitting. The intarsia knitweave breaks up the horizontal colourway and so incidentally does the unusual looped fringing and the three beads slung

Figure 172. Embroidered Knitwoven wall hanging. Brother 840

under the brown knitweave near the top. Knitweave is delightful for wall-hangings. It may be chosen by the non-machine knitting expert because it looks like weaving, but its characteristics could not be more different. It can be picked out immediately as the odd one out in a room full of loom-woven fabrics. Knitweave comes alive with the draught and heat and moves with a gentle, rhythmic fluidity that is rare in loom-woven fabrics of a similar weight. Knitweave curls in a little at the edges, even after crochet has been applied; let it do so. It should also be left without lining. Knitweave can be seamed or it can be hung sideways.

The fringing

This is done by a looped method well known to knitters of long standing. There is an accessory for the Knitmaster 120 known as the drive lace attach-

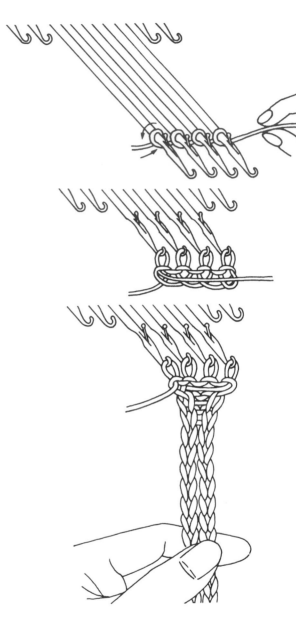

Figure 173. Making a rouleau or cord

ment (Fig. 174). The hook combs are clamped between the machine and the table top to allow a space between the hooks and the needles on the bed. A coloured yarn is then wound round in a criss-cross herringbone fashion from the needleheads to the bar hooks of the comb. There are two ways you can deal with the wrapped yarn:

1. Leave it and the bar in place. Knit the row carefully with the carriage. Push the needles to HP if necessary. This row holds the loops in place, which

Figure 174. Knitmaster 120 and drive lace fabric
(Knitmaster)

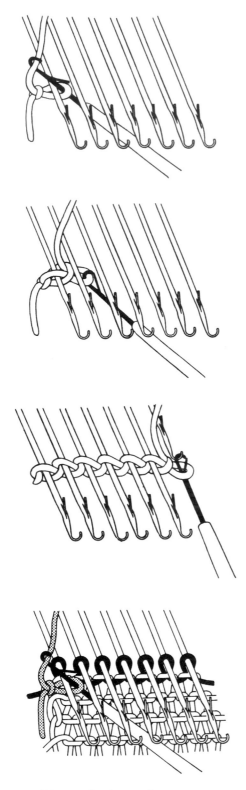

can be cut if you choose. Remove the bar at the end of the row.

2. Slip the stitches previously held by the needles behind the latches. Draw the needles back and knit the row manually over the introduced yarn. When you release the yarn from the hooked comb you will have a long, lacy, open structure, which can be swung into scallops by the selection of needles. This is one of two forms of drive lace that can be done on Knitmaster machines. The other is a double bed variety. On the older machines one used to hold a ruler near the needles and wrap that, edging the ruler along the row as one worked; it did not take long to realise that one could use the Brother and Toyota casting on combs and the Knitmaster lace combs (260–360) on the standard machines What is so useful about this technique is that it can be superimposed onto an existing purlside stitch pattern like knitweave, tuck or slip, for an added dimension of colour, irregular pattern and 3-D textural effect. What is more, one could build layer upon layer in different colours for a separate design following a pattern drawn on the charting device.

Crochet cast on

On the sampler for a wall hanging, to give the top fringe definition, a row of crochet cast on has been worked above it, giving it a braided look. Of course, braids and fringes can be knitted separately, hung on the needles and knitted in. They can also be added afterwards. Embroiderers have turkey stitch and weavers knotted pile. This looped stitch is one machine knit equivalent. A great deal of inspiration can be had from looking at 3-D effects in weaving and embroidery, but one needs a vocabulary of techniques to work knitting translations. The mastery over the machine has one important side benefit. Those who turn their noses up at the machine are shown the inspirational effect it can have on the imagination that is stirred by its use.

Beads

The bottom row of beads on the sampler were threaded on a nylon thread, which was laid across extended needles and the beads poked down between. Then the row was knitted. There is actually nothing gained by knitting-in large beads this way. Small ones benefit more by this method. Beads are best stitched onto machine-knit fabric. One can anchor large beads under a transparent nylon snood, knitted beforehand on the machine (Fig. 176). One can also knit nylon pouches using the knitted-in pocket method. Pop the bead or pebble in the transparent pouch and seal it by placing the bottom and top stitches on the machine and knitting the row.

Figure 175. Diagram showing crochet cast on

Figure 176. Beaded knitting

The sides of the pouch can be stitched up at the end of the knitting.

The slip stitch
This particular one is known as the ridge stitch or tea cosy pattern. Lock card 1 in the basic pack on row 1. Knit 8 rows slip and 2 rows stocking stitch. The pattern has beautiful textural qualities. There is no reason why we cannot use it on a multicolour HP intarsia setting.

The garter bar
British knitters are not as well acquainted with this accessory as are their American counterparts. The garter bar is of course ideal for the removal of ribbed welts from one machine with a ribber to another machine without one. It has in fact, many functions, its most valuable being that it can reverse fabric and put it back on the machine quickly and efficiently. The knitter needs to practise with the garter bar. There is a knack of holding the accessory straight in alignment with the needle shanks while at the same time easing the stitches onto the eyed teeth of the garter bar. When one is expert, whole sections of stitches can be made to move onto the teeth in one simple action. There is a garter bar for the standard 4.5 mm machines, and one for the Knitmaster 120. The garter bar adds another dimension to one's work in both texture and pattern.

Appliqué and 3-D effects
Until machine knitters began to use double bed jacquard on the Passap and on the Japanese machines with confidence, there was no really suitable fabric to knit as an appliqué base. Double bed jacquard has a great advantage over single bed Fair Isle in that all its floats are enclosed. If a medium weight yarn is used, then one in three needles can be put up on the ribber. This gives a more fluid fabric than if all needles were used on the ribber. The wall hanging, 'Star Wars', was done in this way. It was knitted in sections which were seamed invisibly by mattress stitch (Fig. 178).

It is much easier for the owners of the Japanese Electronics, the Passap Duomatic and the Superba, to design jacquard than it is for the punchcard machine owners, for the simple reason that the cards for the former are marked in the same way as for Fair

Figure 177. Handling the garter bar

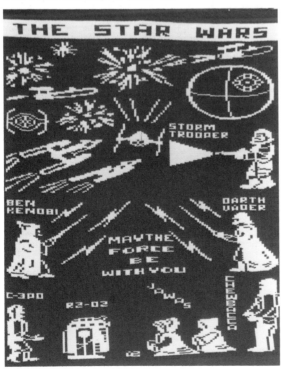

Figure 178. 'Star Wars' by Anne Bayes, Sydney, Australia. Singer (Aus) SK 500. Jacquard setting

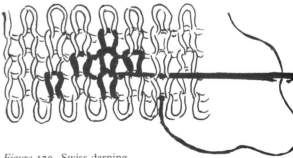

Figure 179. Swiss darning

Isle (single bed). Nevertheless, jacquard will come into its own as more people acquire ribbers and colour changers, and become acquainted with their use.

Jacquard has other advantages:

1. Its edges hang straight and do not curl in at the sides as do knitweave and Fair Isle. Therefore, it does not require lining, or even the addition of a crochet edging.

2. Its surface is ideal for embroidery and stitchery. The top layer of knitted stitches lifts up and makes needlework very easy to accomplish.

3. Its fabric is firm and strong and will take layer upon layer superimposed on it without stretching in the warp or weft.

Figure 180. Autumn fire appliqué

4. Jacquard is ideal for coats, jackets, capes and is the chosen medium of fibre artists, like Susanna Lewis of New York, who are involved in the wearable art movement.

Autumn Fire

All the materials in the 'Autumn Fire' appliqué were machine knitted. The base fabric is jacquard, knitted on the Knitmaster SK 500 (Electronic) with SRP 50 ribber and colour changer (Fig. 181). The slots for the dowelling rods at the top and bottom were done by holding the ribber needles at slip (both levers at 0 on ribber carriage) for 10 rows and then reversing the process. At the end of the pattern the card was programmed on a blank row, and self-coloured jacquard (with one colour) was knitted till the wall hanging was complete.

Punchcard machine owners can take any section of the flame pattern they wish, providing it will fit into the 24 stitch repeat system. If you have a Knitmaster machine then put the blue and orange striped card that is in your colour changer pack underneath a blank punchcard. Brother and Singer Knit Copy owners – punch a master card and lay it over a blank card (Fig. 182). In actual fact Knitmaster owners will also require a master card, because this is needed to

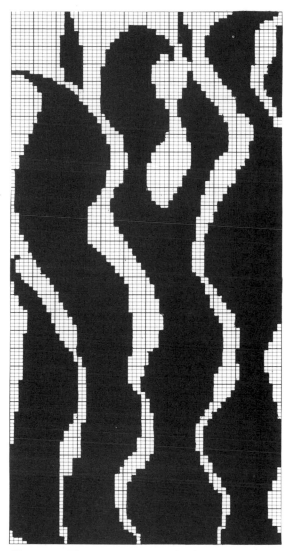

Figure 181. Flames – pattern card for SK 500

knit self-coloured jacquard when the pattern is complete. The jacquard card is punched in a positive and negative row arrangement. The patterning rows are marked in twos and punched first and the background rows are done afterwards. It is not as difficult as it sounds. The instruction manual needs to be followed carefully, but nothing can go wrong if these directions are followed. The background rows go below and above and the holes punched for them complement the ones punched for the patterning rows. Note: For self-coloured jacquard the colour changer is not needed as only one colour is used.

Details of the appliqué

The flames, which act as pale shadowy reflections are,

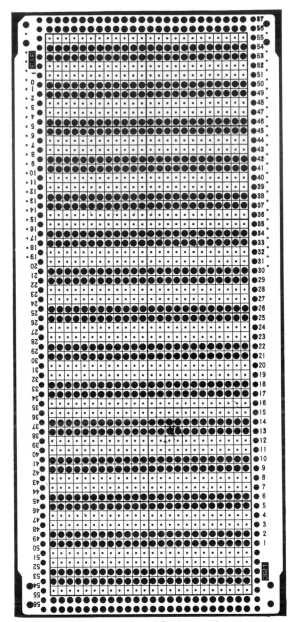

Figure 182. Master punchcard for jacquard

The flames were made to be as varied as possible. If you look in a fire you will see that each flame has a character of its own. What is more, movement is unceasing. It is difficult to catch that in a still-life wall hanging.

Multicoloured Sweater

Machine knitting may be fascinating or useful, or both, but it is great fun as well. The multicoloured sweater celebrates a carefree, do-it-yourself, unconventional approach. The traditional pattern format, therefore has been abandoned. The principles only are given; a stitch by stitch commentary would be required otherwise, and that would fill a book of its own.

Sources of inspiration

There were three sources of inspiration for this garment:

1. The Knitmaster intarsia sideways-knitted, batwing sweater from the 3500 manual. It is interesting that this manual accompanied a British-made machine and that it described unusual techniques like the figure-of-eight graft, which are not known to Japanese knitters. It would appear that the intarsia method and the figure-of-eight graft came directly from the English framework tradition.

2. The cover outfit in issue No. 6, volume 16 of the British edition of the *Knitking* magazine (U.S.A.).

3. The slide featuring a sweater by Connie Cashmere in the interesting *Knitting* slidepack produced by the British Crafts Council. This slidepack is mostly concerned with machine knitted items.

Method of knitting

First, the charting device cannot be used. The simplest possible garment design was the pattern guide. Two rectangles were knitted, one for the back and one for the front. The sleeves were narrowed at the wrist by the HP method. Narrow black hems were added by picking up the stitches on the back, front and cuffs. A row on T 10 was knitted first and this was picked up on the completed hem. Another row on T 10 was knitted and then all the stitches cast off. The shoulders were cut and sewn against a slope of 2.5 cm and a few rows turned in at the top to give a boat-neckline.

Paper patterns

Dressmaker's paper, marked off in centimetres, or half inches if you can still get it, should be the base for the drawing to scale of the back/front and sleeve. As the tension in 3-ply on T 5 was 32 sts – 44 rows per

of course, part of the jacquard pattern. These were done in a dull, wheaten cream acrylic yarn, set in a background of shades of grey/white variegated acrylic yarn. Some of the fabric stitched on was waste. Appliqué provides a marvellous exercise for the discovery of the nature of materials. Other pieces, like the rouleaux and mohair and lurex flames, were specially knitted. Particularly successful were the intarsia knit weave logs, with a crinkly grey bouclé as the main yarn and a smooth silky, thick black as the main weaving yarn.

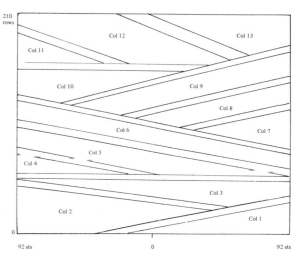

Figure 184. Diagram for back and front of multicoloured sideways knitted top. Begin and end with waste yarn on all 184 stitches, then start holding position pattern. The narrow bands enclose black. Tension: 32 stitches, 44 rows per 10 cm. Tension 5 on Brother 830

Figure 183. Multicoloured top or sweater. Kathleen and Helen Kinder, Brother 830

10 cm, the imperial measure of 8 sts – 11 rows per inch proved the easiest to mark on half inch grid paper. The horizontal measure represented the total length of the garment, and the vertical perpendicular one the width and 5 cm (2 in) ease. The garment (back, front and sleeves) was knitted sideways.

When the width and length are marked off in stitches and rows, draw your lines to mark the enclosure of the colours. Each one is highlighted by bands of black, as in the Connie Cashmere and *Knitking* designs. There were 15 colours in our original here and that included lurex. The bust measurement was 96 cm (36 in) and the garment weighed 375 g (14 oz).

Knitting instructions

Begin and end with waste yarn. If you go hopelessly wrong in your calculations you can always do a complete cut-and-sew. If you relax and enjoy the knitting the odds are that your calculations will be right. It is important to deal with one colour at a time. Estimate the depth and turn it into rows. Look at the baseline and turn the width into stitches. Some of the

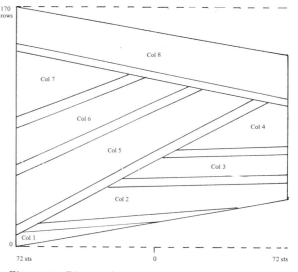

Figure 185. Diagram for sleeve of multicoloured top. Begin and end with waste yarn. Hold all stitches except about three or four at extreme left. The colours may be the same or different from those on the back and front

diagonal stripes will be knitted with needles pushed into HP at one side and then pushed back in stages until the correct width of stripe is achieved. The black edge stripes are mostly knitted straight. There is a little HP shaping at the extreme edges to fit in with the main colours. Try and work out the groups of HP needles as evenly as possible. However, you can always cheat and adjust the numbers when you

Figure 186. Cape/wall hanging – machine knit, crochet, stuffed and padded. Susanna Lewis, New York, U.S.A. Passap Duomatic

notice that the depth of the wedge is going to be too small or too large. The important rule is to see that the garment piece has even and regular measurements. The sides are the places to watch. If the piece is a little narrower in the middle, then you will have a more fitted sweater.

In any event, the result will be a cheerful, eye-catching, fun sweater which looks stunning on a tall, raven-haired girl, wearing tight black pants, black highwayman boots and a black silver studded belt, low slung on the hips.

The Wearable Art Movement

The movement is just beginning to attract comment and exert influence in the U.K., whereas for several years it has caused lively interest in the U.S.A. The point about wearable art is that it has a dual function. The article is meant:

    (a) to be worn and regarded as a piece of clothing, and

    (b) to be looked at and handled as an *objet d' art*, separately, and independent of wearer, usually as a wall-hanging.

This is no doubt an area of controversy and the first point one can make is that the wearer and the article together make the impact. The public are deeply involved and the reception they give to an article of clothing, which may be way-out to them, can affect not only the wearer's attitude to it and to them, but how he or she wears it.

An article hung on a wall, or in a free-standing position, may reveal quite different characteristics than when it is worn. What is controversial is when judges prefer articles for exhibition which can only be shown in this way. Gloves, for example, have traditionally reached the summit of the knitters skill in exquisite art-craftsmanship. They most certainly would fail one of the two fashionable wearable art tests, and so indeed would many beautiful garments whose qualities can only be revealed in the wearing.

There is a strong argument in favour of special-occasion, dramatically different clothes. Most of us are dyed-in-the-wool reactionaries and can be quite cruel to those who choose to assault the senses with garments that are different. There is, however, a growing minority of people who are becoming aware of clothes that have a special, almost unwearable appeal. If the time and the place is right, the clothes are looked at, handled, and enjoyed. What is more, with the public warm in appreciation, the wearer enjoys the experience.

In whatever direction the wearable art movement develops, there is one underlying factor – the compelling urge to gaze at and to handle fibre, yarn and fabric in exciting combinations, in as many different areas of life as possible.

Fashion and fibre art
No attempt has been made in this book to differentiate between fashion and highly individual wearable art. If the latter succeeds in capturing an exclusive market and invites imitators, then it has become fashion of a rather rare sort. This occurrence is far from uncommon and it suggests that there are quite a few potential customers who are rebelling against mass production and are longing to express their individuality by purchasing and wearing 'one-off' creations.

All this underlines the wisdom of Japan in the support she is giving to domestic, craft and industrial knitters alike. After all, the knitting schools of the Yorkshire and Cumbrian Dales sustained a knitting industry in England, which lasted for well over three hundred years.

10 Yarns and the charting device

Two factors have revolutionised the machine knitting scene in recent years. One is the usage of coned yarns, both industrial and branded, and the other is the growing practice of charting device knitting. Though one can consider these under separate headings, yarn and the charting device are inter-related. The growing popularity of the charter is due in no small way to the arrival of a variety of yarns, which no longer knit to standard tension on a stocking stitch setting, though one can indeed classify them roughly as 1-ply, 2-ply, 3-ply, 4-ply and so on. There is a third factor, and that concerns the growing sophistication of the modern machine and its ability to produce a host of stitch patterns with a bewildering variety of stitch and row tensions. No pattern writer could possibly satisfy the needs of a machine knitter faced with such choice, though patterns are rich sources of ideas and inspiration.

The Yarns

It is valuable to mention briefly:
(a) the kind of yarns readily available in coned yarn centres and through mail order, and
(b) the yarns used in patterns in this book.

While yarns provide the raw material, they also are a powerful commercial weapon. Some machine knitters in one or two parts of the English speaking world are concerned about the lack of coned yarns available to them and the exorbitant prices they are asked to pay for what there is. Naturally, these knitters are also concerned about the poor rate of growth in the machine knitting craft. As far as the lack of coned yarns is concerned, it may simply be that machine knitters form too small a part of the knitting community to make the production of coned yarns a viable proposition.

With the growing popularity of machine knitting in the U.K. we are witnessing a determined effort to pull machine knitting back into the hand knitting camp. While many machine knitters knit with yarn prepared for hand knitting from time to time, there are good reasons why balled hand knitting yarn cannot ever assume the importance it had in the 1960s and early 1970s:

(a) Balled yarns are too expensive for machine knitters who use up yarn much more quickly than their hand knitting counterparts.

(b) Balled yarns do not go as far as industrial or specially prepared coned yarns.

(c) Having to stop and cope with knots is irritating and time consuming.

(d) It is also a waste of time to have to wind and wax hand knitting yarn.

(e) Some yarns for hand knitting produce stiffish, unyielding garments even when knitted on the correct tension on the machine.

(f) The growing interest in yarn mixing and sampling provides for much more creativity in the production of the garments than the use of a commercially prepared single end of yarn.

(g) Though patterns are still bought with as much enthusiasm as ever, the charting device takes away the dependence of the knitter on the written pattern. It is this which marks quite sharply the difference in attitude and practice of the hand and the machine knitter.

Japan

In Japan more than half the households have a knitting machine. There is no anti-machine movement in the crafts and hand and machine knitting co-exist very happily; I have already discussed in the previous chapter the Japanese long-term commit-

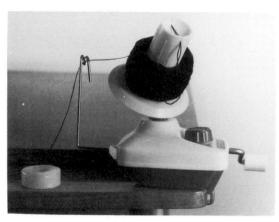

Figure 187. Wool winder and wax ring

Figure 188. Section of yarn-mix top. Stocking stitch and tuck. Passap Duomatic with Deco. Card 17

tronics, when they are given a chance to use them. The yarn-mix textured top pattern at the end of this chapter was devised and knitted by a twelve-year-old, who found hand knitting difficult.

When you consider how much mechanical and electronic equipment you deal with competently in your daily lives, it is nothing short of insulting to be told you haven't the intelligence to use a knitting machine. It is not surprising to learn that many women succumb to such powerful psychological weaponry used to great effect in the yarn war. William Morris would be pleased to know that his anti-machine movement in the crafts still goes on kicking after a century of influence. Knitting machines go under beds, on top of wardrobes, or are advertised for sale in the columns of newspapers, but if you are determined not to be brainwashed you will get out the machines and use them. If you need help, a dealer or importer will tell you of books, magazines and clubs. Many local education authorities run classes for machine knitters in Adult Education Centres. Before you realise it, the obnoxious thing has become the source of the greatest possible pleasure, and is useful into the bargain. After all, hand knitting authorities are only protecting their interests in putting you off the machine. It is their job to see that their kind of yarn and its end product always stay to the forefront of the fashion and craft activity arena. To date, this amounts to nothing less than a very considerable business success story, but whether it allows for the fullest possible development of the knitting craft is a matter of the greatest possible doubt.

What is fashion and shows signs of remaining so could have considerable impact on future developments in Japanese knitting machine technology. There are European firms with a stake in the standard machine market who would be only too pleased to increase their share, should the Japanese show any signs of losing their dominance.

As a matter of fact, there are major disadvantages to the Japanese dominance. The branded yarns used exclusively by Japanese knitters may be varied but they tend to be balled. The yarns fall into two main categories: (1) heavy, for hand knitting and for chunky machine knitting, (2) finer, for standard machine knitting and for use by a minority of hand knitters, who still like to knit with 2- 3- and 4-ply yarns. Should the branded yarn companies wish to withdraw their patronage and cease to produce the kind of yarn most machine knitters require, then one can imagine that interest in the craft will decline rapidly. Since finer plies in ball form are more expensive to produce and their profit return con-

ment to building up an influential, international knitting and fashion industry, but there are other reasons. To Western hand knitting authorities who claim that machine knitting only maintains a static growth, it should be pointed out that in Japan machine knitting flourishes, as hand knitting does in the U.K., under the heavily subsidised patronage of the branded yarn companies. In the U.K., for example, the machine knitting craft may be small, but it owes its liveliness and creativity to individual entrepreneurs. Moreover, Japanese women do not appear to find machine knitting difficult, as it is often claimed British women do. It is interesting to see how easily our young people in the U.K. take to knitting machines, especially to the Passap and to the Elec-

siderably less than on chunky, brushed or fancy yarns, this development is not beyond the bounds of possibility. One alternative is a more concentrated promotion of the 'simple' chunky machines, which indeed have their place, but which can in no way hope to recover and revitalise, as the standard machines are doing, the fine hand-knitting traditions of days gone by. Fortunately, the future of mainstream machine knitting looks more promising than this.

Though machine knitting activity in the U.K. and in the U.S.A., as well as in other parts if the English speaking world, is small compared with that in Japan, its potential for growth is enormous. Moreover, in the West there are not only signs of a truce in the yarn war, but some evidence that a few major yarn companies are giving considerable thought as to how best they can serve the existing machine knitting market. There are signs of a closer relationship between hand and machine knitting, now that it is being realised that each activity can complement the other. A significant minority do both hand and machine knitting, though to the majority of machine knitters hand knitting is a painfully slow, time wasting and limiting exercise when the machine holds out greater and speedier rewards. If a knowledge of hand knitting is a help and not a hindrance, then equally it is necessary to have some understanding of what is going on in the field of industrial knitting and yarn manufacture, and some knowledge of the availability of its expertise and products.

Industrial counts of yarn

Most of the industrial yarns at present sold by coned yarn suppliers have a 2 on the top line of what looks like a fraction. Just a 1 represents singles, so a 2 represents a doubles – two strands twisted together to form one. $\frac{2}{8}$ is a common 4-ply equivalent industrial Shetland. If the 2 is the count or ply, then the 8 refers to the number of industrial hanks to the pound. The more hanks there are the higher the number and the finer the yarn. The yardage in the hank varies according to the yarn and is determined by an industrial table for different yarn types. Since this system is being overtaken by others it is futile to go into details. What is important is how the yarn knits on the domestic machine.

Yarns available to the knitter

Quite a few machine knitters in the U.K. have reasonable access to a coned yarn centre. Many more deal very happily with mail order firms, which advertise in the machine knitting and needlecraft press.

1. *Synthetic and synthetic mixes*

(a) There are 2- 3- and 4-ply coned yarns available. Some are acrylic while others are acrylic-nylon-wool mixes. This is a particularly important group to American knitters who tend to use more synthetic yarn than pure wool on the machine. In the U.K. 4-ply acrylic is by far the most popular and cheapest but there is a special place for a 3-ply acrylic-nylon. The lacy summer blouse shown earlier was knitted in coned 3-ply acrylic-nylon. These are all branded yarns and are sold on cones of 340, 350 and 500 g make-ups. The yarns are also supported by pattern literature. Yarns used for the rib tuck head hugger, the embroidered stockings with clox and the raglan top and skirt come into this category. Recently, the choice of these yarns has been increased by the arrival of a double-knitting coned acrylic. This yarn was used for the hat and mitts set.

(b) Fine industrial acrylics or acrylic mixes are mostly industrial surplus yarns on cone, though $\frac{2}{30}$, which is the most popular of this group, can be had as a repeatable yarn. This we call a $1\frac{1}{3}$ ply equivalent as 3 ends make a standard 4-ply. Fine counts are much sought after by knitters who do yarn mixing and double bed knitting. The acrylic wools used in the plated tuck cardigan and some of the fine yarns in the appliqué and sampler come into this group. Another popular fine yarn is $\frac{2}{24}$ bright acrylic. Two ends of this can be used as a 3-ply equivalent.

(c) Fancy yarns cover a whole host of yarns – brushed acrylics, mock mohair, slubs, bouclés, poodles and knop yarns, to mention but a few. Some fancy yarns are offered by branded spinners as repeatable lines and on cones of between 250–300 g. Others are industrial surplus and it is difficult to classify them, except by trying them out on the machine. These are excellent used on their own or in a yarn mix, as in the top discussed under the charting device.

2. *Wool*

In recent years wool has recovered some of the ground it lost to acrylics. The traditional methods of wool processing were not only costly, but they added considerably to pollution problems. Now processes have been speeded up and pollution dangers minimised. Moreover, the dwindling supply of oil has meant increased costs in the production of acrylics and other man-made fibres resulting in the narrowing of the price gap between them and natural fibres like wool.

(a) 4-ply Superwash on cone

This is usually a top quality Superwash branded yarn on 400 g cones and is a favourite with machine knitters who knit top quality wool garments. A 3-ply is available, but it is not as common. Occasionally one comes across good quality wool-nylon mixes, again mostly in 4-ply.

(b) Industrial top-quality wools

In the last few years the recession has made it possible for top quality industrial repeatable wools to be sold in coned yarn centres. They range from reasonably-priced to quite expensive. It is too early to say what kind of a long term impact these wools will make, but already top quality industrial wools are showing every sign of carving out a place for themselves in the growing range of yarns used by machine knitters.

The most common are $\frac{2}{16}$ (2-ply) English and Border Crossbreds, but top quality Botany $\frac{2}{13}$ (2-ply) or $\frac{2}{24}$ (1$\frac{1}{4}$-ply) Superwash are also making an appearance. The $\frac{2}{13}$ Botany is usually on cones of 200 g, but the other wools come on large factory cones of around 1$\frac{1}{3}$ kg from which some dealers are only too happy to wind off customer requirements. The $\frac{2}{13}$ and $\frac{2}{24}$ make superb jacquard and lace yarns. The traditional jersey design was knitted using 3 ends of $\frac{2}{16}$ crossbred, which made a substantial, warm fabric.

(c) Oiled Shetland-type wool

This is oiled, industrial short-stapled wool, most of which has never been near the Shetland Isles. It is a popular yarn because it is wool and cheap at the price. One or two enterprising spinners offer Shetland as a branded yarn, but mostly it is available as non-repeatable industrial wool. Shetland is most commonly sold in $\frac{2}{14}$, $\frac{2}{10}$ and $\frac{2}{8}$ counts.

$\frac{2}{14}$ = 2 ply equivalent. Knits on T5 for stocking stitch.

$\frac{2}{10}$ = 3 ply equivalent. Knits on T7 for stocking stitch.

$\frac{2}{8}$ = 4 ply equivalent. Knits on T8 for stocking stitch.

Because this wool is in oil, it is knitted on at least one whole number higher than its ply equivalent. The sample is then washed, dried and pressed. Any tendency to harshness will have disappeared and the fabric becomes soft and attractive. The sleeveless Fair Isle waistcoat was knitted in $\frac{2}{14}$ oiled Shetland yarn.

(d) Oiled lambswool

This is softer wool than Shetland. Usually lambswool is available as a $\frac{2}{19}$ 2-ply equivalent. It should be treated as oiled Shetland, as should oiled Botany on cone, if you can get it. Lambswool mixes very well with fine acrylic-nylons, poodles, bouclés and even fine, bright acrylics. Two ends of lambswool make a substantial 3-ply equivalent.

3. *Speciality yarns*

These could be of natural fibres like silk, cotton, cashmere, alpaca, angora or mohair, or yarns for unusual effects like chenille (the fine variety) or lurex.

Regenerated fibres like rayon are not as popular as formerly. Rayon is a beautiful yarn, but it can produce problems for the knitter. It rubs up when on needles in holding position, and it is heavy and has a tendency to drop. Cotton, incidentally, has a tendency to shrink. (Tessa Lorant has dealt very fully with speciality yarns in *The Batsford Book of Hand and Machine Knitting*).

Most high quality speciality yarns are in balls or on small cone make-ups. Industrial equivalents can sometimes be had, but it is usual to buy this type of yarn from a specialist retailer. Occasionally knitters use branded balled yarns when they wish to follow a specific pattern. Hand knitting qualities are usually kept for the heavy gauge knitting machine on the market. In recent years hard wearing British yarns like Herdwick, Swaledale, Black and Grey Welsh and Jacobs have been knitted by machine Knitters on the chunky machines. $\frac{2}{8}$ qualities are also available in some of the native wools, which are economically priced. The $\frac{2}{8}$ variety makes lovely fisherman's rib sweaters, but these wools tend to be hairy. Brushes should be kept clean on the carriage, and a hand vacuum taken over the bed of the machine when the garment is complete (Fig. 190).

Real Shetland from the Shetland Isles is available as 2-ply jumper weight (4-ply equivalent) and 2-ply lace weight. This beautiful wool is a favourite with craft knitters for traditional and picture knit sweaters and is available direct from the Shetland Isles.

This short guide can barely do justice to the wide variety of effects knitters are achieving with threads as well as with yarns. In fact, we are most fortunate to have so much so readily available, and it is this profusion which will enable the craft of machine knitting to expand.

Yarn mixing and sampling

Though the majority of garments knitted are from branded coned yarns, using a single end, there is growing interest in yarn mixing and sampling amongst knitters who would have never considered it as an option previously. Knitters are beginning to experiment with texture and the contrast of yarn, thread and pattern. There is no need to mix the yarns first if you would prefer to knit them as separate ends. Knitmaster have a device called the twister which will twist two or three ends together in interesting mixes (Fig. 192). You can make your own device. A simple three-tier vegetable rack is most useful. Place one cone on the bottom shelf; thread the end from this cone up through the middle of the second cone which you place in the second level. The two ends are

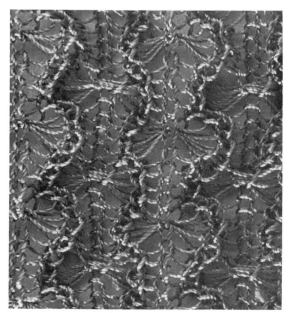

Figure 189. Guipure lace stitch pattern (in rayon). Passap Duomatic

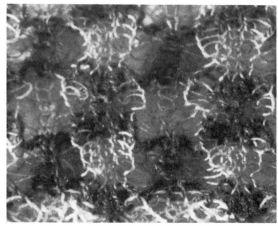

Figure 191. Rib tuck with Mohair/acrylic and threads. Passap Duomatic Deco card 17

Figure 192. Knitmaster twister (Knitmaster)

Figure 190. Knitwoven wall hanging using handspun Jacob's and Suffolk wools. The commercial varieties are Shetland, Herdwick, Swaledale and Cheviot. Knitmaster 326

then threaded up through the middle of the third cone placed on the third level. The end from this will twist naturally round the other two as the triple-ended yarn is fed through the yarn mast.

Yarn recipes

$\frac{2}{14} + \frac{2}{10}$ = fine double knitting (T8 or St S 8).
$2 \times \frac{2}{30}$ + fine bouclé = heavy 4 ply (T7.2 or St S $6\frac{3}{4}$).

Fine bouclé on its own on the stocking stitch setting produces a row and stitch relationship like tuck i.e. few stitches and many rows per 10 cm.

Yarn tip

This only seems to work when the denominator is

divided by 8. Take $\frac{2}{16}$ (2 ply), $\frac{2}{24}$ ($1\frac{1}{3}$ ply) and $\frac{2}{32}$ (1 ply). Share the denominator by 8. Thus, $16 \div 8 = 2$, so 2 strands of $\frac{2}{16}$ are equivalent to $\frac{2}{8}$ (4 ply). Share 24 and 32 by 8 in the same way and you will require 3 and 4 strands respectively to make up the $\frac{2}{8}$ weight. $3 \times \frac{2}{30}$ on the other hand appears to work best as a fine 4-ply and not as a $\frac{2}{10}$ (3-ply). There are indeed problems associated with the constituents of the yarn, how it is spun and whether it is hairy, shiny, smooth, textured, etc. Trying to equate ply with count has only limited value. Experimenting with yarns on the machine and writing down suitable stitch sizes seems to be the only answer.

Yarn counts – some metric conversions

The commonest industrial yarns used are classified as worsted counts (WC). Here are some metric conversions.

Imperial	Metric
$\frac{2}{8}$	$= \frac{2}{9}$
$\frac{2}{10}$	$= \frac{2}{11.3}$
$\frac{2}{16}$	$= \frac{2}{18}$
$\frac{2}{24}$	$= \frac{2}{27}$
$\frac{2}{30}$	$= \frac{2}{34}$

The formula is as follows. Multiply the denominator of the imperial count by $\frac{34}{30}$. Thus, $\frac{2}{16}$ is $16 \times \frac{34}{30} = 18$. The metric worsted count is therefore $\frac{2}{18}$.

Guide for stitch tensions

Figure 193 is a rough guide to the tensions one may achieve in stocking stitch on a common group of yarns.

The Charting Device

The Knitmaster Knitradar was the first charter to appear in the UK in 1972. The KR 5 was not the original one but its successor, which appeared in 1973–4. The essential features have been retained in more recent models.

At first there was considerable opposition to the use of the charting device amongst knitters and designers not only in the West but also in Japan, where it originated. The interesting point is that the traditional method of following a written pattern, prepared by a pattern writer from a diagram block, translated into rows and stitches, was at most only thirty or so years old. In the past, when knitters could not read, shape was all-in-all. A garment was measured with the eye and the span of the hand, and immediately the knitter began to translate the visual image and the meagre information gained by the hand into stitches and rows.

Up to the early 1950s diagrams were included with hand knitting patterns and hand knitters were shown how to make their own linear patterns by leading authorities like Mary Thomas and James Norbury. Modern hand knitting authors also instruct their readers on how to work from a pattern chart but, as far as branded patterns are concerned, in the early 1950s the diagrams suddenly disappeared. Knitters were guided entirely by the written word. The machine knitters followed the hand knitting format until the late 1950s, when diagrams and diagrammatic methods began to appear in European magazines. The magazines were produced by firms like Passap and then, later in the 1960s, by Knitmaster and Jones in the U.K. It must be said, however, that British knitters never took to an exclusively diagrammatic format. It is only comparatively recently that many Passap knitters in the U.K. have found themselves at home with the Passap Model Book approach.

It is the older knitters who have problems; younger knitters have grown up with diagrammatic methods of working. After all, information fed through the media as well as through our education system comes to us very largely by charts and visual line images. Their efficiency in communication is unquestioned.

There is no doubt that the written pattern format has contributed greatly to the commercial success of the British branded yarn spinners, though their counterparts in Europe seem to flourish as well with annotated diagrams. More recently, however, concern has been expressed in hand knitting quarters about the lack of young people who are taking up the craft. It is feared that the momentum of recent years will not be maintained. Hand knitters, like machine knitters before them, are beginning to wonder if a more efficient means of pattern communication cannot be found than the bewildering, abbreviated code of a written pattern.

Diagrams, on the other hand, are the means of instant recognition. To judge by the growing number of English speaking machine knitters who subscribe to Japanese language publications, the diagram and the metric system provide a lingua franca of increasing international importance. As far as machine knitters are concerned, the charting device holds the key to this success. What is most interesting is that Japanese magazines devoted to hand and machine knitting expect hand knitters to knit by diagram as well.

The Passap system

For years, Passap knitters have followed their own system of chart instruction supported by written text

Ply	Stitches per 10 cm	Rows per 10 cm	No. of stitch Dial	Stitch size (Passap)
2	25–38	48–52	3–4	4–5
3	32–34	44–48	4–5	5–6
4 (fine)	29–31	40–44	6–7	$5\frac{1}{2}$–$6\frac{1}{2}$
4 (heavy)	27–28	37–40	7–8	6–7
DK (fine)	25–26	32–36	8–9	$6\frac{1}{2}$–$7\frac{1}{2}$
DK (heavy)	22–24	30–31	9–10	8

Figure 193. Guide to stitch tensions

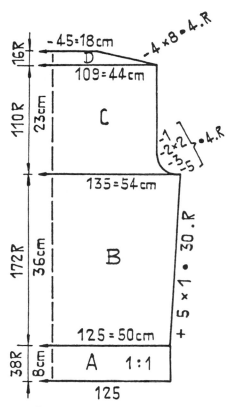

Figure 194. Passap diagram. (Passap, Switzerland)

containing essential information. A sketch of the garment is presented, carefully labelled with necessary measurements and shaping instructions in a simple code. The Passap system revolves round the row and stitch readings of a 100 stitch–100 row swatch. All information detailed on the sketch proceeds from the swatch. The row and stitch data are read off the Passap charts in the instruction book.

Many experienced knitters prefer this way and still are unwilling to let the charting device show them where, when and how much to shape and knit. In the Passap system the measurements required are worked out beforehand and written on a sketch of the pattern. It is a remarkably speedy way of knitting once it is mastered and understood. If the charter had nothing further to offer then there would be no reason for change. In actual fact, the Passap system can be a most useful aid in some shaping processes using the charting device.

The Japanese charting device system

All knitting to size involves the correct measurement and reading of a tension swatch, and tension is crucial no matter what system you use. Unlike the Passap system, the Japanese method proceeds from a swatch with essential measurements taken from between 40 stitches and 60 rows. This ratio is chosen for the simple reason that, on average, the width of a stitch in proportion to its length is 2-to-3. There are two systems relying on this swatch method.

(1) The half size, half scale charters. The Knitmaster Knitradar, Passap Forma and Superba Pattern Driver follow this approach. The reading is based on 10 cm. Knitmaster owners use the little green ruler to measure the distances between the stitch and row markers, while the Passap and Superba knitters select the 10 cm readings from the charts provided for swatches of 100 stitches and 100 rows.

Since there are occasions when it is useful for all knitters to knit a 100 stitch–100 row swatch, a chart has been compiled of all 10 cm readings that occur most often with these swatches (Fig. 196). Look for the measurement your swatch has achieved, first in width and then in length, and read down for the 10 cm reading. If you have a little green ruler you can use it as a counter check. Mark the beginning and end

133

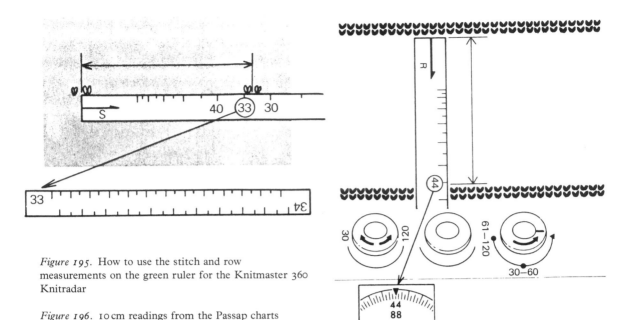

Figure 195. How to use the stitch and row measurements on the green ruler for the Knitmaster 360 Knitradar

Figure 196. 10 cm readings from the Passap charts

Fig. 196

For test squares measuring 10 to 19.5 cm

cm	10	10.5	11	11.5	12	12.5	13	13.5	14	14.5	15	15.5	16	16.5	17	17.5	18	18,5	19	19.5	cm
10	100	95	91	87	83	80	77	74	71	69	67	65	63	61	59	57	56	54	53	51	10

For test squares measuring 20–29.5 cm

cm	20	20.5	21	21.5	22	22.5	23	23.5	24	24.5	25	25.5	26	26.5	27	27.5	28	28.5	29	29.5	cm
10	50	49	48	47	45	44	43	43	42	41	40	39	38	38	37	36	36	35	34	34	10

For test squares measuring 30–39.5 cm

cm	30	30.5	31	31.5	32	32.5	33	33.5	34	34.5	35	35.5	36	36.5	37	37.5	38	38.5	39	39,5	cm
10	33	33	32	32	31	31	30	30	29	29	29	28	28	27	27	27	26	26	26	25	10

For test squares measuring 40–50 cm

cm	40	40.5	41	41.5	42	42.5	43	43.5	44	44.5	45	45.5	46	46.5	47	47.5	48	48.5	49	49.5	50	cm
10	20	25	25	24	24	24	23	23	23	22	22	22	22	22	21	21	21	21	20	20	20	10

of 60 rows and mark the twenty-first needle on either side of 0 during the knitting of the 100 stitch–100 row swatch. All swatches should be pulled lengthways and widthways and then left to relax before being stab pinned (without stretching) onto a carpet or polystyrene tile for measuring. If you press or steam then do it before measuring.

Two readings can be taken, one with the green ruler and the other from the chart of 10 cm readings. The results should, of course, be identical.

(2) The metric measurement between 40 stitches and 60 rows. The full scale, half and full size charters, Brother Knitleader, Toyota Knit Tracer and Singer Knit Copy follow this principle. The stitch and row

formulae for translation from method 1 and vice-versa are given in the pattern notes for the plated tuck cardigan but, very simply, they are as follows for Brother, Toyota and Singer owners. If you wish to find the 10 cm readings you work out:
(i) The number 400 shared by the measurement between 40 stitches, (ii) The number 600 shared by the measurement between 60 rows.

In the patterns in this book, the two different swatch readings are given to accommodate all charting device owners.

Stitch tension and fabric construction

A few guidelines can be given but, ultimately,

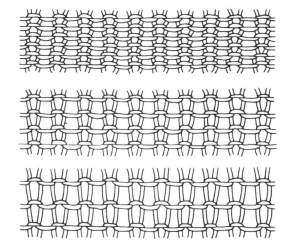

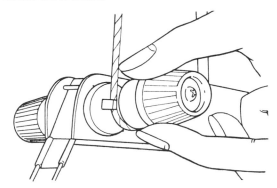

Figure 197. How to find the right stitch tension. The middle one is correct

Figure 198. Adjusting the yarn brake tension

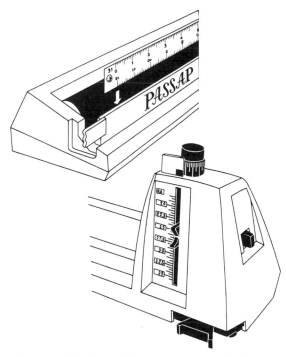

tension is too loose. Similarly, if the stitches appear as hard little knots in the needle heads, the tension is too tight. A good fabric is springy without being too floppy or too hard. Yarn, stitch size and pattern contribute to texture; all four, nicely balanced, produce a perfect construction.

How the charting device works

All charting devices are devised to work on similar lines.

1. Each has a set of stitch rulers, the half scale charters have two sets. The set with 0 in the middle is for asymmetrical shapes. The ruler is chosen according to the stitch reading.

2. Each has a row click-on mechanism which is geared to the reading selected by the knitter from the measurement on the swatch.

3. Each has a clutch system which is a safety device for the row mechanism. Always see that the charter is out of action and not clicking on when it is not required.

4. Either a paper pattern is used as with the half scale charters, or one is drawn onto a plastic sheet in the case of the full-scale charters.

Some hints and tips

1. Always check all measurements before using the pattern block if it is a commercial one. It is no use blaming the charter for not knitting correctly when

Figure 199. The full-scale, full-size Brother Knitleader

experience is the only teacher as to whether the tension chosen is too tight or too loose. The tension on the yarn brake must also be just right; it is often forgotten in the quest for a good fabric construction. Look also at the stitches hanging on the needles. If there is too much space between the bottom of the stitch and the needle head then the odds are that the

Figure 200. The Passap Forma row scale and locking lever (bottom) and the Passap Forma stitch scale

Figure 201. The built-in Knitleader on the Brother 881

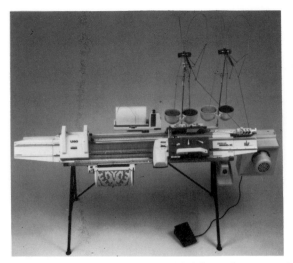

Figure 202. The Passap Duo 80 with full attachments. (Passap, Switzerland)

you never made a check for accuracy at the start.

2. Check your own pattern measurements yet again.

3. Always read the charter at the right and take it in two row runs. In a symmetrical piece cast off the same number at the left as you cast off at the right and do not read the charter again until you return the carriage to the right.

4. If the line of the block moves down and strikes between the stitch markings you must decide whether to shape or not to shape. Whatever you decide the charting device will eventually show a clear-cut amount, and half a stitch left to be cast off or on till the next time round is neither here nor there.

5. On some row and stitch tensions the charter does not click on in regular amounts. The use of the human calculator is needed (in conjunction with an electronic one sometimes) to sort out the decreases into large, then graduating to proportionately smaller, amounts if a curve is being shaped. For a raglan the stitch decreases need to be worked out as evenly as possible.

Two misconceptions about the charting device

1. The charter does not cast on or cast off for you. Your hands perform the operation required in obedience to the line of the block striking the stitch ruler, as the sheet advances into the attachment.

2. The charter offers no help when you are sideways knitting and using the holding position for shaped pieces. If the charter revolved on an axis you could use it for the multicolour sweater, for instance.

The importance of the charting device

The bulk of knitting is done in a vertical direction from bottom to top. For this the charting device is a brilliantly conceived aid, so simple, yet as clever and as useful as cats' eyes on the road. Speed is certainly one of its greatest assets. Experienced knitters will claim that they can do the same with sums on a bit of paper, a familiar system and a calculator. It may be so for a well-tried conventional garment, but it is doubtful whether knitters using traditional methods can move with such speed and facility between stitch patterns, garment shapes and yarn weights of great diversity as can charting device knitters. Because the charter relieves the knitter of so many chores, she is free to handle and sample a greater variety of yarns than ever before.

The great contribution of the charting device is that it enables machine knitters to deal with the majority of patterns efficiently. The knitters who must read and then knit, and whose knitting is punctuated by frequent stops to read the next lot of instructions, to decipher the next series of symbols on an annotated diagram, must proceed more slowly. The charter makes it easier to concentrate on the essential knitting task. For the first time you can stand back from row and stitch analysis and consider form and line and the relationship of shape to colour, yarn, texture and stitch pattern. The Japanese have taken the process a stage further. Their designers show the basic block within the pattern that they have created from it. The evolutionary process of design deserves a book to itself (Figs 203–204); it is one that is just beginning to excite Western knitters. In the pattern following we start with the simplest of shapes in the most interesting of industrial yarn mixes. You may also wish to consider why knitters in colder climates are more interested in fabrics of pronounced texture than those who live in or near the Tropics!

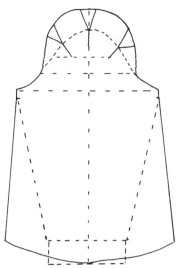

Figure 203. The development of a full sleeve with puffed sleeve head from a standard block

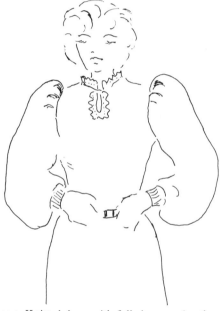

Figure 204. Knitted dress with full sleeve and gathered sleevehead

There is still a need for some pattern writing but this is mostly for the discussion of techniques and suggestion of possible alternatives. It is a pattern format that will come, but not yet, not until everyone has a charting device. Every manufacturer whose sales are worldwide has a charting device attachment that will fit the machines in his current range. One point of real significance is that Brother have now joined Knitmaster in marketing a machine, the 881, that has a built-in charter. No greater recognition could be given to the importance of the charting device.

Textured Overtop

Measurements
To fit loosely size 87 cm (34 in). Actual measurement 97 cm (38 in).

Materials
Total weight 675 g (23 oz) cream poodle (acrylic-nylon), cream $\frac{2}{30}$ acrylic, fine bouclé, coffee-coloured. 0.5 m (20 in) of cord elastic.

Figure 205. The textured overtop. Kathleen and Helen Kinder, Knitmaster 326

Tension
27 stitches – 39 rows on T8.1 (Passap St.S $7\frac{1}{4}$) 14.8 cm per 40 stitches, 15.4 cm per 60 rows. Reversed stocking stitch side used.

Machine
Knitmaster 326.

Charting device instructions (in order)
The actual measurements to be drawn for the block are given. Half scale charter owners (Knitradar, Forma and Pattern Driver) should halve the measurements for their block. These follow in brackets.

1. Draw AB 71 cm (35.5).
2. Mark AX depth of shoulder 3 cm (1.5).

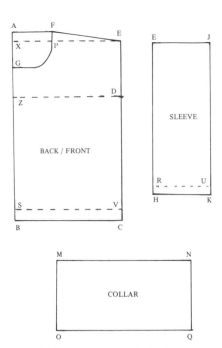

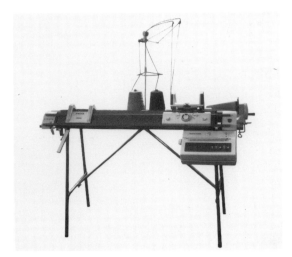

Figure 207. The Singer (Superba) Electronic 2310

2. Width: half of total 19.5 cm (9.75).

Knitting notes

Hems: COBH 'e' wrap over eon. Turn up and hitch on eon on completion of hem. Tension for hem same as MT. Mark under arm at D with WY. Hold stitches on neck and shoulders. Graft shoulders on completion. Graft neck stitches to collar side edge. Start and finish collar with WY. Graft together first and last row. Remove WY. Knit cord over four needles for bottom edge, using $3 \times \frac{2}{30}$. Insert cord elastic in sleeves. Do not press.

The charting device format

Space has been given to step-by-step instructions for drawing a simple block. The actual knitting notes are brief compared with those required for a written pattern. The block can be used again and again and the garments that result will each be different according to the yarn and stitch pattern that you choose. Perhaps we are looking at the shape of things to come and the beginnings of a revolution in our knitting habits.

There can be very few crafts in which the craftsman puts together the raw materials in a highly individual combination to construct the fabric of his choice to use in a personalised garment design. In this alone machine knitting can take up where the handloom weaver of the past left off. Machine knitting ought to be regarded as the craft which produces the stuff of modern life and all nonsense about it being too difficult, a non-craft and the destroyer of originality forgotten once and for all.

Figure 206. Half-width charting device blocks for textured overtop. N.B. purl side is right side

3. Mark AG depth of front neck 12 cm (6).

4. Mark XZ armhole depth 26 cm (13).

5. Draw BC quarter of total bust 24.25 cm (12.125).

6. Draw XE across shoulder, parallel and equal to BC 24.25 cm (12.125).

7. Join EC equal and parallel to XB 68 cm (34).

8. Draw AF half of back neck 9.5 cm (4.75).

9. Join shoulder FE.

10. Mark ED armhole depth, equal and parallel to XZ 26 cm (13).

11. Draw half front neck curve from G to F GT = half AF 4.75 cm (2.375).

Curve up to P. PF is straight and parallel to AX.

12. Mark SB depth of hem 5 cm (2.5). Join SV.

N.B. The depth of hem is knitted twice. Roll back the sheet to BC for fold row and repeat.

Sleeve

1. Draw centre length EH 54 cm (27).

2. Draw half circumference HK 26 cm (13).

3. Complete rectangle draw EJ and KJ.

4. Mark depth of hem RU 2.5 cm (1.25).

Collar (knitted from side to side)

1. Length: MO 59 cm (29.5).

Appendices

Abbreviations

alt	alternate
altog	altogether
beg	begin
carr	carriage
CO	cast off
COBH	cast on by hand
cm	centimetre(s)
col	colour
cont	continue
dec	decrease
DK	double knit
eon	every other needle
FI	Fair Isle
Fig of 8	Figure of eight
foll	following
ff	fully fashioned
g	gramme(s)
HP	holding position
in	inch
inc	increase
J & B	Jones and Brother
k	knit
MB	Main bed
mm	millimetre(s)
MT	main tension
MT − 1	main tension minus one whole number (example)
MT + 1	main tension plus one whole number (example)
MY	main yarn
n	needle
NWP	non-working position, or A position (Japanese machines)
opp	opposite
oz	ounce
PC	punchcard
RB	rear bed
rem	remaining
r	row
RC	row counter
SD	selector dial
st	stitch (abbreviation never used after 1)
St s	stitch size (Passap)
T	tension (on stitch dial – Japanese machines)
tog	together
UWP	upper working position
WP	working position
WY	waste yarn

Distributors

U.S.A.

Contact the following distributors for product information and dealer referrals.

Associated Knitting Machine Co.
1275 Bloomfield Ave.
Fairfield, NJ 07006
Distributes Passap and Superba east of the Mississippi

Bernina Sewing Machine Co., Inc.
70 Orchard Dr.
North Salt Lake, UT 84054
Distributes Passap west of the Mississippi

Brother International Corp.
8 Corporate Pl.
Piscataway, NJ 08854
Distributes Japanese single-bed machines

Kimberly Market Corp.
3900 Brinton Pl.
Charlotte, NC 28226
Distributes the single-bed Bond Knitting Frame

Knitking
1128 Crenshaw Blvd.
Los Angeles, CA 90019
Distributes Knitking, Genie, Corona, and other knitting machines; publishes Knitking *magazine specifically for machine knitters*

Leclerc Corp.
P.O. Box 491
Plattsburg, NY 12901
Distributes Superba west of the Mississippi

Singer
135 Raritan Center Pkwy.
Edison, NJ 08837
Distributes Japanese single- and double-bed machines

Studio Yarn Farms, Inc.
10001 14th Ave., S.W.
P.O. Box 46017
Seattle, WA 98146
Distributes a number of Japanese Silver-Seiko single- and double-bed machines

Toyota Knitting Machines
c/o Newton's Knits, Inc.
3969 East La Palma
Anaheim, CA 92807
Distributes Japanese single-bed machines

CANADA

Leclerc Impex, Inc.
104 5th Ave,
CPO 69, L'Isletville
Quebec GOR 2Co
Distributes Superba in Canada

Singer Company Canada, Ltd.
200 St. Louis
St. John
Quebec Q3B 1Y1
Distributes Japanese single- and double-bed machines

White Elna
1470 Birchmount Rd.
Ontario M1T 2G1
Distributes Passap in Canada

Resources

The Machine and Hand Knitters Directory
LRH Enterprises
c/o The Knitting Machine Studio
42 Hillside Avenue
Englewood, NJ 07631

The Knitting Guild of America
P.O. Box 1606
Knoxville, TN 37901
Publishes Cast On: The Magazine for Knitters

Further Reading

Anthony, Jane. *Machine Knitting – Practical Guide.* MacDonald and Jane, London, 1977

Anthony, Jane. *Machine Knitting 2 – More Creative Ideas.* MacDonald and Jane, London, 1979

Faust, Regine. *American Indian Designs Adapted to Knitting.* Regine Studio Knit Designs, Toronto, 1979

Faust, Regine. *Fashion Knit Course Outline.* Burgess Publishing Co., Toronto, 1978

Faust, Regine. *Tuck Knitting.* Regine Studio Knit Designs, Toronto, 1979

Gartshore, Linda. *The Craft of Machine Knitting.* Hutchinson, London, 1978 Merrimack Publishing Circle

Hampton, Pat. *Blocking for Machine Knitters.* Route 1, Box 98-D, Paeonian Springs, VA 22129

Hampton, Pat. *Common Sense Fitting for Machine Knitters.* Route 1, Box 98-D, Paeonian Springs, VA 22129

Holbourne, David. *The Basic Book of Machine Knitting*. Van Nostrand Reinhold, New York, 1979

Holbourne, David. *The Book of Machine Knitting*. [Batsford, London, 1979] David and Charles

Kinder, Kathleen. *The Passap Duomatic, Deco and Forma*. The Dalesknit Centre, Settle, Yorkshire, 1981

Kinder, Kathleen. *A Resource Book for Machine Knitters* (Nos. 1 and 2). The Dalesknit Centre, Settle, Yorkshire, 1983

Kinder, Kathleen. *A Resource Pattern Book Supplement for Machine Knitters*. The Dalesknit Centre, Settle, Yorkshire, 1983

Lorant, Tessa. *Hand and Machine Knitting*. Scribners, New York, 1981

Lorant, Tessa. *Yarns for the Knitter*. The Thorn Press, Somerset, England, 1981

Nobuyuki, Tami. *Knitting Machine Workbook* (Nos. 1, 2, and 3). P.O. Box 4284, Whittier, CA 90605

Norman, Mary Louise. *Nicely Knit Lines*. 1310 Clermont Street, Denver, CO 80220–2440

Ratcliffe, Hazel. *Machine Knitting*. [Pan, London, 1978] State Mutual Books

Raymond, Jodie. *Let's Knit Some Blouses*. P.O. Box 8631, Jacksonville, FL 32211

Raymond, Jodie. *Let's Knit Some Skirts*. P.O. Box. 8631, Jacksonville, FL 32211

Raymond, Jodie. *A Shirt for All Seasons*. P.O. Box 8631, Jacksonville, FL 32211

Raymond, Jodie. *Signature Hats and Caps*. P.O. Box 8631, Jacksonville, FL 32211

Raymond, Jodie. *Upside Down Raglan Pullovers for Everyone*. P.O. Box 8631, Jacksonville, FL 32211

Raymond, Jodie. *V-Neck Raglan Upside Down Sweaters for All*. P.O. Box 8631, Jacksonville, FL 32211

Schneider, Joyce. *Fairisle Yokes, An Addendum*. 106 Shady Nook Avenue, Catonsville, MD 21228

Schneider, Joyce. *Yoke Sweaters and Easy Way*. 106 Shady Nook Avenue, Catonsville, MD 21228

Smith, Mariette. *Custom Charting*. Vol. I. 2146 Michigan Road, Port Huron, MI 48060, 1984

Smith, Mariette. *The Custom Fit in All You Knit*. 2146 Michigan Road, Port Huron, MI 48060, 1984

Smith, Mariette. *Designer Dresses*. Vols. I and II. 2146 Michigan Road, Port Huron, MI 48060, 1983

Smith, Mariette. *Designer Tops*. Vol. I. 2146 Michigan Road, Port Huron, MI 48060, 1983

Smith, Mariette. *Knitting Machine Techniques*. Book I. 2146 Michigan Road, Port Huron, MI 48060, 1981

Smith, Mariette. *Patterns for the Whole Family*. 2146 Michigan Road, Port Huron, MI 48060, 1982

Sweet, Norma. *Chart-Rite*. 8222 24th Street Court West, Tacoma, WA 98466

Sweet, Norma. *Curves, Curves, Curves*. 8222 24th Street Court West, Tacoma, WA 98466

Sweet, Norma. *That Final Touch*. 8222 24th Street Court West, Tacoma, WA 98466

Weaver, Mary. *Japanese for Machine Knitters: An Aid to Reading Japanese Patterns*. Weaverknits, Dartford, Kent, England

Weaver, Mary. *Machine Knitted Skirts*. Weaverknits, Dartford, Kent, England, 1982

Weaver, Mary. *Machine Knitting Technology and Patterns*. Weaverknits, Dartford, Kent, England, 1980

Weaver, Mary. *The Passap Duomatic*. Weaverknits, Dartford, Kent, England, 1974

Weaver, Mary. *The Ribbing Attachment;* Parts I and II. Weaverknits, Dartford, Kent, England, 1974–76

NOTE: Many of the books listed above may be obtained from:

Alles Hutchison, 315 Hamil Road, Verona, PA 15147
The Knitting Machine Studio, Inc. P.O. Box 746, Englewood, NJ 07631

See also the list of retail dealers in *The Machine and Hand Knitters Directory*

Magazines and Periodicals
Cast On: The Magazine for Knitters
The Knitting Guild of America
P.O. Box 1606
Knoxville, TN 37901

Fashion Knitting
In Crafts, Inc.
155 Avenue of the Americas
New York, NY 10013

Knitting Machine Digest
Hazel Ratcliffe
c/o The Knitting Machine Studio
P.O. Box 746
Englewood, NJ 07631

Knitting Machine News and Views
Alles Hutchison
315 Hamil Road
Verona, PA 15147

Machine Knitters Newsletter
130 West 29th Street
Third Floor
New York, NY 10001

Vogue Knitting
P.O. Box 1072
Altoona, PA 11603

Manufacturers' Periodicals for Machine Knitters:
Knitking Magazine
1128 Crenshaw Blvd.
Los Angeles, CA 90019

Passap Model Books:
Inquire of Passap importers listed on page 140

Japanese Periodicals:
Knitting Fashion Monthly
Silver-Seiko Ltd.
16–6 Shinjuku 2 Chome
Tokyo 160
Japan

Nihon Vogue Publications
34 Inchigaya-Honmuracho
Shinjuku-Ku
Tokyo 162
Japan

Slide Pack:
Knitting (mostly by machine) from:
The Crafts Council
12 Waterloo Place
London SW1Y 4SU
England

Brand Names of Knitting Machines

Silver-Seiko machines are imported from Japan and sold by the following companies under their brand names:

U.K.
Knitmaster – Empisal

U.S.A.
Studio

Canada, Australia, New Zealand
Singer

The Knitradar is known as the Knitcontour in the U.S.A.

Index